I0518089

52 WEEK PRAYER & DEVOTIONAL

by

Dr. Patricia L. Harris

52 WEEK PRAYER & DEVOTIONAL

by

Dr. Patricia L. Harris

52 Week Prayer & Devotional

Harris, Patricia 2024
52 Week Prayer & Devotional / Dr. Patricia L. Harris
ISBN: 979-8-9868620-9-5 (pbk)

Book Layout and E-book Design by:
sugarray@sugarraydestin.com

FIRST PAPERBACK EDITION

Printed in the United States of America 10 9 8 7 6 5 4 3 2

Dedication

This book is dedicated in memory of my son,
Mr. James E. Matthews,
who influenced countless people in his too short time here on earth.
Oh, how I miss you.
Thank you for believing in your mom.
You told me that I was strong and courageous.
You believed in me, and I will always love you.
Son, you had a big heart.
You loved family and friends, always putting a smile on our faces.
Your memories will be treasured by all the lives you touched.

CONTENTS

Introduction

The burden of a missing child. I decided to write this devotional, because my faith in God kept me during the most difficult time of my life. It only takes a phone call or a knock on the door, and your life will never be the same.

It was the Word of the Lord that got me through the most challenging season of my life. Prayer sustained me. I made daily affirmations, believing God that my son would be found. Intercessors around the globe were praying for my son to be found. I decided to talk about the burden of a missing child. The pain was excruciating. My heart was crushed. There were so many unanswered questions.

I wrote the 52 Week Devotional with scriptures, prayers, and affirmation. There is comfort for those who are grieving. My emotions, guilt, depression, anger, sadness, and anxiety had to be processed.

I found hope through my spiritual faith in the Lord.

This devotional and journal has been prepared to guide you through grief, loss, hope, and recovery. Embrace a message of hope and inspiration. Know that healing is possible. Honor your loved one's memory, and rediscover joy and purpose in your life. Even in the midst of a tragic, dark moment, there is a flicker of light at the end of the tunnel. Connect with the Lord, and allow the healing process to begin.

My son was found, and he was deceased. The search lasted 10 months and 10 days. My mind was being tormented during the wait. It was the Word of God and prayer that kept me. My favorite scripture is Psalm 119:105, “Thy Word is a lamp unto my feet, and a light unto my path.”

God is the best source of comfort. Put Your trust in Him.

WEEK 1: *Burden*

DAY 1: *Burden*

"But in my distress, I cried out to the Lord; yes,
I prayed to my God for help. He heard me from His sanctuary;
my cry to Him reached His ears."
Psalm 18:6

PRAYER:

Lord, my heart is very heavy. My child has not come home. Lord, I pray that you will protect him. Lord, you know where my child is. Please keep him safe. I pray to hear good news soon. Thank you, Lord. Amen.

AFFIRMATION:

I have faith that this will all work out.

DAY 2: *Burden*

"Be of good courage, and He shall strengthen your heart, all ye that hope in the Lord."
Psalm 31:24

PRAYER:

Lord, I am trusting You to do a miracle. Lord, my child is missing. Lord, strengthen me on this journey. Lord, I put all of my trust in You.

AFFIRMATION:

Today, I exude strength, grace, and flexibility.

DAY 3: *Burden*

""Come to me, all who are weary and heavy-laden, and I will give you rest."

Matthew 11:28

PRAYER:

Today is a new day. I have now faith. I am believing, God, that this too shall pass. My child will return home safe. Do this for my family, Lord. This is my prayer. Amen.

AFFIRMATION:

Today, I choose to give God my worries and burdens. For He cares for me.

DAY 4: *Burden*

"Casting all your cares upon Him, for He careth for you."
1 Peter 5:7

PRAYER:

Lord, I know you hear my prayers. I am asking you to take care of my missing child. Every day I become more and more concerned. I ask for Your protection for my loved one. Lord, I am depending on You during this crisis. My family is in need of You, Lord. Amen.

AFFIRMATION:

I am grateful for the people I have in my life.

DAY 5: *Burden*

"Never worry about anything. Instead, in every situation, let your petitions be made known to God through prayers and requests, with thanksgiving. Then, God's peace, which goes far beyond anything we can imagine, will guard your hearts and minds in union with the Messiah Jesus."

Philippians 4:6,7

PRAYER:

Lord, I thank you for this day. I am giving you all the praise today because you are in total control. Lord, my situation is still the same. We don't have any answers. Lord, we cast all of these burdens to You today.

AFFIRMATION:

I breathe in healing. I exhale the painful things that burden my heart.

DAY 6: *Burden*

"Cast your burden on the Lord, and He shall sustain you;
He shall never permit the righteous to be moved."
Psalm 55:22

PRAYER:

Dear Lord, it's a new day. I give You the praise, Lord. My prayer today is for the welfare of my family. We are waiting in great expectation of a major breakthrough. Lord, we are praying for the whereabouts of my dear child. Lord, let us hear good news. We are believing and hoping for a breakthrough in Jesus' Mighty Name. Amen.

AFFIRMATION:

In spite of my circumstances, today is a great day.

DAY 7: *Burden*

"The Lord deserves praise! Day after day, He carries our burdens, the God who delivers us. Our God is a God who delivers; the Lord, the Sovereign Lord, can rescue from death."
Psalm 68:19-20

PRAYER:
Dear Lord, Thank you for Your loving kindness. You have been so good to me and my family. You are my burden-bearer. I cannot carry this burden alone. Thank you, Lord. Amen.

AFFIRMATION:
I cast every burden on Christ, today. Lord, set me free.

WEEK 2: *Hope*

DAY 8: *Hope*

""Why am I discouraged? Why is my heart so sad?
I will put my hope in God! I will praise Him again – my Savior and my God!"
Psalm 42:11

PRAYER:
Dear Lord, we are hoping to hear good news today. Lord, we thank You for all the love and support that we are receiving from around the world. Lord, we thank You during this difficult season in our lives. Our hope is in You. Amen.

AFFIRMATION:
Hope is a choice; I choose to be hopeful.

DAY 9: *Hope*

"You are my refuge and my shield. Your Word is my source of hope."
Psalm 119:114

PRAYER:
Lord, we are thankful for this beautiful day. We are hoping that the telephone will ring and we will hear the news we are hoping for. Lord, You are our help and our hope is in You. Amen.

AFFIRMATION:
I choose hopefulness.

DAY 10: *Hope*

"Let Your unfailing love surround us, Lord, for our hope is in You alone."

Psalm 33:22

PRAYER:

Dear Lord, each day we hold firm to our hope that is in Christ Jesus. May the Lord bless you abundantly with rest for the heart, power for virtue, patience in suffering, and wisdom for life. May the Lord bless you with joyful hope in taking one day at a time. Amen.

AFFIRMATION:

I hold onto hope.

DAY 11: *Hope*

"Faith shows the reality of what we hope for; it is the evidence of things we cannot see."
Hebrews 11:1

PRAYER:

Lord, I am Your humble servant. I come before You today in need of hope. I pray for hope. I need hope to believe that our child will be found. I trust You, Lord, with all that's on my heart. You are the hope for the hopeless. I give You praise and I say thank you, Lord. Amen.

AFFIRMATION:

My hope is a powerful force.

DAY 12: *Hope*

""I am counting on the Lord; yes, I am counting on Him.
I have put my hope in His word."
Psalm 130:5

PRAYER:

Oh Lord, look upon all Your people around the world who have a child that is missing. Lord, we are hurting. Our hearts are heavy. Remind us of Your invitation, "Cast all your cares upon me", and of Your assurance. Lord, Your words let us know that You care for us. We thank you Lord. Amen.

AFFIRMATION:

Today, I am hoping for the best concerning my loved one. I will control my emotions and thoughts.

DAY 13: *Hope*

"I say to myself, The Lord is my inheritance; therefore, I will hope in Him!"
Lamentations 3:24

PRAYER:
Lord, Your Word says You are the hope for the hopeless, so I'm running to You and grabbing onto You. Lord, today, help us to bask in Your glory. God, you are my hope and I trust You. Amen.

AFFIRMATION:
Problems are opportunities. My hope is in the Lord.

DAY 14: *Hope*

"So be strong and courageous, all you who put your hope in the Lord!"
Psalm 31:24

PRAYER:
Dear Lord, in this season of trial, I ask for Your strength to bring hopefulness into my life once more. Lord, this is a storm for sure. Lord, You are my strength that I can depend on. Lord, I know that You can calm the storm. This is my prayer for hope in Christ Jesus. Amen.

AFFIRMATION:
I will always have hope.

WEEK 3: *Brokenhearted*

DAY 15: *Brokenhearted*

"The Lord is close to the brokenhearted; He rescues those whose spirits are crushed."

Psalm 34:18

PRAYER:

Today, I will give You praise, Lord. I am thankful for all of my blessings. I am thankful and grateful for everything. Our hearts are hurting as we await an answer. I will continue to magnify the Lord, even in this difficult time. A heart of gratitude and thankfulness. Amen.

AFFIRMATION:

I am letting go of all of my pain. I am healing and moving forward.

DAY 16: *Brokenhearted*

"He heals the brokenhearted and bandages their wounds."

Psalm 147:3

PRAYER:

Dear Jesus, today I surrender my broken heart to You. I ask You to comfort me and my family. Jesus, I know that You are a healer. I have faith that You are healing me and my family. Jesus, put the pieces back together like only You can. Amen.

AFFIRMATION:

Today, I am choosing happiness, healing, and freedom.

DAY 17: *Brokenhearted*

""The Lord hears His people when they call to Him for help. He rescues them from all their troubles. The Lord is close to the brokenhearted; he rescues those whose spirits are crushed."

Psalm 34:17-18

PRAYER:

Dear Lord, I thank You that You are healing my broken heart. Today, I pray for strength. Thank You for giving me the strength to do all the things that I was able to do. Lord, You are working things out for my good. Amen.

AFFIRMATION:

I am a positive person. My healing process has begun.

DAY 18: *Brokenhearted*

"You keep track of all my sorrows. You have collected all my tears in Your bottle. You have recorded each one in Your book."

Psalm 56:8

PRAYER:

Lord, I am so thankful to see a new day. My prayer focus is "Create in me a clean heart, Oh, God, and renew a steadfast spirit within me". Search my heart, Oh Lord; if there be any wickedness, pull it out of me. Lord, heal my heart completely. Amen.

AFFIRMATION:

My heart is healing. I trust that I will recover.

DAY 19: *Brokenhearted*

"My health may fail, and my spirit may grow weak,
but God remains the strength of my heart; He is mine forever."
Psalm 73:26

PRAYER:

Lord, this has been a rough time for me. The tears keep flowing. I will put all of my confidence in the Lord. For all things are working together for my good. For You know what the outcome may be. It shall work for my good. Amen.

AFFIRMATION:

I am healing, and I am happy.

DAY 20: *Brokenhearted*

"Their insults have broken my heart, and I am in despair.
If only one person would show some pity; if only one would turn and comfort me."
Psalm 69:20

PRAYER:

Lord, heal my heart and fill me with joy again. Lord, I have lost my joy because of the things that have happened. Help me to rejoice. For this is Your will for me. Amen.

AFFIRMATION:

I will be gentle with myself today. I will allow my heart to be healed.

DAY 21: *Brokenhearted*

"A glad heart makes a happy face; a broken heart crushes the spirit."

Proverbs 15:13

PRAYER:

Lord, my heart is broken. This pain has shattered my heart. Let not depression overtake me. Make me whole again. Wipe away all of the tears from my eyes. Touch my heart, oh Lord. May I be restored fully. Amen.

AFFIRMATION:

Today, I choose to have a grateful heart.

WEEK 4: *Grief*

DAY 22: *Grief*

"I weep with sorrow; encourage me by Your Word."
Psalm 119:28

PRAYER:
Dear Lord, I thank You for this amazing day. I ask for Your comfort to overwhelm me right now. Help me process what I am going through, Lord. I am trusting You will be with me every moment while I go through this. Lord, help me to keep my eyes on You. Thank You, Lord. Amen.

AFFIRMATION:
Today, I am holding onto love and letting go of grief.

DAY 23: *Grief*

"So with you, now is your time of grief,
but I will see you again and you will rejoice,
and no one will take away your joy."
John 16:22

PRAYER:

Lord, I thirst for You even as the tears flood my face. Lord, You are my refuge and strength, a present help in the time of trouble. I am grieving for my loved one to be found. My heart is heavy. My tears continue to fall down my face. Take my heartache and pain. Lord, You are in control. In Jesus' Name, Amen.

AFFIRMATION:

I allow myself to feel my grief and then let go.

DAY 24: *Grief*

"Blessed are those who mourn, for they will be comforted."
Matthew 5:4

PRAYER:

Lord, You know my affliction. Help me keep my heart open to Your Holy Spirit. Lord, I know that You care for me. Lord, thank You for the comfort I find in the knowledge that You know what I am going through. Comfort me, Lord. Amen.

AFFIRMATION:

I am finding strength in myself as I grieve.

DAY 25: *Grief*

"Long ago, the Lord said to Israel: I have loved you, my people, with an everlasting love. With unfailing love, I have drawn you to myself."

Jeremiah 31:3

PRAYER:

Lord, You are my strength like no other. We need You, Lord. Give us the strength to go through this storm. Our hearts are heavy. Lord, You have shown Your loving kindness towards us. Help me to find peace in Your presence. Amen.

AFFIRMATION:

I choose to heal my hurt spirit.

DAY 26: *Grief*

"'For the mountains may move, and the hills disappear,
but even then my faithful love for you will remain. My covenant of
blessing will never be broken,' says the Lord who has mercy on you."
Isaiah 54:10

PRAYER:

Lord, I thank You for this day. Thank You that I am not alone. You are always with me. Lord, You are faithful. Thank You for Your compassion that never fails me. Thank You for Your enduring peace and Your presence. Amen.

AFFIRMATION:

I am discovering new strengths within myself.

DAY 27: *Grief*

"Then, Jesus wept."

John 11:35

PRAYER:

Lord, I am finding it so hard to even get up out of bed to start the day. I ask You to touch my hurting heart. You are the God of all comfort. Please dry my tears and comfort me today. Amen.

AFFIRMATION:

I am human, and it's okay to grieve.

DAY 28: *Grief*

"Give all your worries and cares to God, for He cares about you."

1 Peter 5:7

PRAYER:

Dear Lord, I bring every grieving parent into Your Throne of Grace. Lord, they are going through a lot of pain. Help them to remain faithful to You even through the pain. Lord, we are seeking answers. Oh, Lord, come to our rescue. We are hurting and we need You. Amen.

AFFIRMATION:

I release grief.

WEEK 5: *Trauma*

DAY 29: *Trauma*

"'Lord, help!' they cried in their trouble, and He saved them from their distress.
He led them from the darkness and deepest gloom; He snapped their chains.
Let them praise the Lord for His great love and for the wonderful things He has done for them. For He broke down their prison gates of bronze; He cut apart their bars of iron."
Psalm 107:13-16

PRAYER:

Lord, God, I pray that You will comfort me in my suffering. Lord, I put all of my trust in You. May Your healing hand rest upon me. Lord, You are faithful. You are going to heal me. Thank You, Lord. Amen.

AFFIRMATION:

I will transform negative experiences into something positive.

DAY 30: *Trauma*

"Those who live in the shelter of the Most High will find rest in the shadow of the Almighty. This I declare about the Lord: He alone is my refuge, my place of safety; He is my God, and I trust Him."

Psalm 91:1-2

PRAYER:

Lord, I pray that you will encourage me throughout the day. Lord, You are with me. It is a dark hour. I have cried and cried. Your Word tells me weeping may endure for a night, but joy is coming in the morning. Amen.

AFFIRMATION:

I am changing in positive ways.

DAY 31: *Trauma*

"I have told you all this so that you may have peace in Me. Here on earth, you will have many trials and sorrows. But take heart, because I have overcome the world."

John 16:33

PRAYER:

Touch me, oh Lord, and fill me with Your light and Your hope. I surrender to You.

AFFIRMATION:

I choose to love myself today.

DAY 32: *Trauma*

"But You are a tower of refuge to the poor, Oh Lord, a tower of refuge to the needy in distress.
You are a refuge from the storm. And a shelter from the heat.
For the oppressive acts of ruthless people are like a storm beating against a wall."
Isaiah 25:4

PRAYER:

Dear Lord, I ask that You would comfort our hearts. Help us to trust the Lord for our healing process. Help us to keep our minds on Christ Jesus. Lord, let miracles of healing happen for Your people around the world. Heal them from all trauma and give them new hope for their lives and future. Amen.

AFFIRMATION:

I choose to make healthy choices.

DAY 33: *Trauma*

"My hands have made both heaven and earth; they and everything in them are mine. I, the Lord, have spoken! I will bless those who have humble and contrite hearts. Who tremble at My word."

Isaiah 66:2

PRAYER:

Lord, we thank You for this day. Each day is a gift from You. Lord, our prayer is for mental healing. So many of us are suffering from trauma. Lord, remove any lies that we have believed. Lord, help us to release all shame and guilt. Lord, heal the mental wounds of the broken. Touch their affliction with Your healing hands. We give You praise for doing it in Jesus' Mighty Name, Amen.

AFFIRMATION:

I will experience peace and joy.

DAY 34: *Trauma*

""But He was pierced for our rebellion, crushed for our sins.
He was beaten so we could be whole. He was whipped so we could be healed."
Isaiah 53:5

PRAYER:

Lord, today is an awesome day. We give You praise. Lord, nobody knows our struggles like You. Give us the strength to move forward this day. Fill us with the peace and joy I know can only come from You during this hard time. I know that with You all things are possible. In Jesus Christ's Name, Amen.

AFFIRMATION:

I am grateful for the love I have received from family and friends.

DAY 35: *Trauma*

"But all who listen to me will live in peace, untroubled by fear of harm."

Proverbs 1:33

PRAYER:

Dear Lord, we ask You to wrap us up in Your love today. We place our problems in Your hand. Lord, we surrender to You all of our hurt, pain, worry, and fear. We release it in Your compassionate care. Amen.

AFFIRMATION:

I receive inner peace today.

WEEK 6: *Stress*

DAY 36: *Stress*

""Trust in the Lord with all your heart; do not depend on your own understanding. Seek His will in all you do, and He will show you which path to take."

Psalm 3:5-6

PRAYER:

Lord, I need Your help. I ask that You will help me to take care of the temple you have given me. I ask You, dear Lord, to heal me and grant me health. Lord, You are my healer. Amen.

AFFIRMATION:

I will not be stressed out by things I cannot control.

DAY 37: *Stress*

"Have compassion on me, Lord, for I am weak.
Heal me, Lord, for my bones are in agony. I am sick at heart. How long, oh Lord,
rescue me? Return, oh Lord, and rescue me. Save me because of Your unfailing love."
Psalm 6:2-4

PRAYER:

Lord, thank You for being my strength and shield. I know that You are a present helper in the time of my circumstances. I know that You are a faithful God. Amen.

AFFIRMATION:

I inhale peace and exhale stress.

DAY 38: *Stress*

"But when I am afraid, I will put my trust in You."
Psalm 56:3

PRAYER:

Lord, You have given me Your peace and calmness. I do not have to accept stress. I put my trust in You, dear Lord. I will not allow my heart to be troubled. Lord, let my heart be filled with joy, peace, and tranquility. Amen.

AFFIRMATION:

I am resilient. I will get through this difficult time.

DAY 39: *Stress*

"When doubt filled my mind, Your comfort gave me renewed hope and cheer."

Psalm 94:19

PRAYER:

Lord, I am reminded that You are with me always. I will not be afraid. Lord, I feel stress and anxiety from life's circumstances. Help me to know that I am secure in You. Amen.

AFFIRMATION:

I focus my energy on my values. I release all stress.

DAY 40: *Stress*

"The Lord Himself will fight for you. Just stay calm."
Exodus 14:14

PRAYER:
Lord, thank You that I can rely on You to fight all of my battles. Stress and anxiety must subside. Lord, fill me with Your peace, today. I give my stress, anxiety, and fears to You. May Your perfect love cast out all fear and stress in my life. Amen.

AFFIRMATION:
I choose positive and nurturing thoughts.

DAY 41: *Stress*

"Put on all of God's armor so that you will be
able to stand firm against all strategies of the devil."
Ephesians 6:11

PRAYER:

Lord, help me not to become anxious about the things around me that I cannot control, but in every situation I face, through prayer and supplication, help me to remember that I am safe and secure when I put my hope in You. Amen.

AFFIRMATION:

I have the power to make positive changes in my life.

DAY 42: *Stress*

"Don't be afraid, for I am with you. Don't be discouraged, for I am Your God.
I will strengthen you and help you. I will hold you up with my victorious right hand."
Isaiah 41:10

PRAYER:
Lord, I thank You that I am anchored in You. I give my stress to You. So that I may find rest for my weary soul. Lift my burdens and lighten my heavy load. Amen.

AFFIRMATION:
I am capable of getting through tough times.

WEEK 7: *Forgiveness*

DAY 43: *Forgiveness*

""People who conceal their sins will not prosper,
but if they confess and turn from them, they will receive mercy."
Proverbs 28:13

PRAYER:
Lord, please help me to forgive those who have hurt me. Help me to release them into Your hands, and heal the wounds of my heart. I choose to forgive all who have hurt me. I pray that You would cover these hurts in Your healing grace, and, through Your strength, empower me to forgive others. Amen.

AFFIRMATION:
I can forgive myself as I forgive others.

DAY 44: *Forgiveness*

"Instead, be kind to each other, tenderhearted,
forgiving one another, just as God, through Christ, has forgiven you."
Ephesians 4:32

PRAYER:
Dear Lord, I do not want to carry this pain any longer. I don't want to be bitter. I am choosing to forgive everyone involved concerning this crisis. "Create in me a clean heart, oh God." Thank You for the gift of forgiveness. Help me to demonstrate Your love even to those who hurt me. Amen.

AFFIRMATION:
I choose to release every painful thought.

DAY 45: *Forgiveness*

"Make allowance for each other's faults, and forgive anyone who offends you.
Remember, the Lord forgave you, so you must forgive others."
Colossians 3:13

PRAYER:
Dear Lord, I come to You today asking forgiveness of all of my sins. Lord, I am thankful for Your forgiveness. Help me to forgive all who have sinned against me. Help me to release the offense out of my mind. Thank You for Your everlasting forgiveness. Amen.

AFFIRMATION:
I am worthy of God's healing power.

DAY 46: *Forgiveness*

"Then, if my people who are called by my name will humble themselves
and pray and seek my face and turn from their wicked ways,
I will hear from heaven and will forgive their sins and restore their land."
2 Chronicles 7:14

PRAYER:

Dear Lord Jesus, please help me to forgive every person who has hurt me. Take the burden of unforgiveness and bitterness away from me. I am willing to forgive them. I am ready to forgive them. I surrender all of my unforgiveness to You. Thank You, Lord. Please forgive me. Amen.

AFFIRMATION:

I forgive all who have hurt me.

DAY 47: *Forgiveness*

"Oh Lord, You are so good, so ready to forgive,
so full of unfailing love for all who ask for Your help."
Psalm 86:5

PRAYER:
Lord, I thank You for Your goodness. Lord, Your Word reminds us to be kind to one another. I need Your strength, dear Lord. Help me to let go of all anger. To forgive is to love and to be free. Lord, have mercy on me and help me to be a forgiving person. Amen.

AFFIRMATION:
Forgiveness gives me a fresh start.

DAY 48: *Forgiveness*

"Now, repent of your sins and turn to God, so that your sins may be wiped away."

Acts 3:19

PRAYER:

Dear Lord, I run into Your open arms. My heart is torn and crushed. I release the pain and sorrow I'm feeling right now. Lord, I have to forgive those who have hurt me. Lord, as I forgive those who caused me unnecessary pain, Lord, I ask for Your peace right now. I need Your peace. Amen.

AFFIRMATION:

I make peace with anyone who has wronged me.

DAY 49: *Forgiveness*

"Where is another God like You, who pardons the guilt of the remnant overlooking the sins of his special people? You will not stay angry with your people forever, because You delight in showing unfailing love."
Micah 7:18

PRAYER:

Dear Lord, our sins are too heavy to carry, too real to hide. Set us free from everything that we cannot change. We humbly confess our sins and ask Your mercy. Lord, I extend forgiveness to all who have hurt me. Lord, I ask to forgive everyone I consider to be my enemy. Lord, I am free from the evil of unforgiveness. Let Your Holy Spirit fill me with light and let every dark area of my mind be enlightened. Amen.

AFFIRMATION:

Each day is a new opportunity to forgive.

WEEK 8: *Depression*

DAY 50: *Depression*

""Even when I walk through the darkest valley, I will not be afraid,
for You are close beside me. Your rod and Your staff protect and comfort me."
Psalm 23:4

PRAYER:

Dear Lord, I am praying for everyone that is battling depression. Lord, this is not easy for us. We are struggling to keep our heads above water. Lord, You are our refuge and hope. Lord, You know our circumstance or situation. We need Your help. We are in desperate need. Amen.

AFFIRMATION:

I work on myself daily.

DAY 51: *Depression*

"The Lord is a shelter for the oppressed, a refuge in times of trouble."
Psalm 9:9

PRAYER:

Lord, it's a new day. I am thankful that You allowed me to see a beautiful day. Lord, I am hurting and the pain is real. I'm feeling overwhelmed to the point where I feel as if I'm shutting down. Lord, I need You to strengthen me right now. Lord, thank You for Your love and peace during this difficult time. Amen.

AFFIRMATION:

Where there is life, there is hope.

DAY 52: *Depression*

"'Comfort, comfort my people,' says Your God. Speak tenderly to Jerusalem. Tell her that her sad days are gone and her sins are pardoned. Yes, the Lord has punished her twice over for all of her sins. Listen! It's the voice of someone shouting, 'Clear the way through the wilderness for the Lord. Make a straight highway through the wasteland."

Psalm 40:1-3

PRAYER:

Lord, I turn to you today. My heart cries out to You. I stand in need of You. Lord, I am asking for deliverance and restoration in my life. Guide my steps to those you have chosen to help me during this season of darkness. Lord, I trust that You are going to bring me out. Amen.

AFFIRMATION:

I am valuable.

DAY 53: *Depression*

"But those who trust the Lord will find new strength. They will soar high on wings like eagles. They will run and not grow weary. They will walk and not faint."
Isaiah 40:31

PRAYER:

Lord, I thank You for this time. Even in the midst of pain and struggle, I know that You are with me. Thank You that You haven't forgotten me and never will. Forgive me, Lord, for not trusting You as I should. I choose to set my eyes on You. Give me the courage to do what I need to do. I am nothing without You. Amen.

AFFIRMATION:

Life is worth living despite my pain and sadness.

DAY 54: *Depression*

"The thief cometh not, but for to steal, and to kill, and to destroy: I am come that they might have life, and that they might have it more abundantly."
John 10:10

PRAYER:

Lord, help me to look to You and You alone to find an abundant life. Lord, I may be in a dark place, but You are able to rescue me. Lord, You have a plan for my life. Help me to see beyond my troubles. The plan that you have for my life is the plan that I surrender to. Please help me to submit to Your plan. You promised me an abundant life. Amen.

AFFIRMATION:

I am strong, and I am an overcomer.

DAY 55: *Depression*

"Three things will last forever - faith, hope, and love - and the greatest of these is love."
1 Corinthians 13:13

PRAYER:

Lord, You are the Way, the Truth, and Life. Thank You, Lord, that You are my hope. While I'm searching for Your light, help me to hold onto You. For You are the light of this world. Lord, show me the light of Your presence. Amen.

AFFIRMATION:

Depression does not have control over me.

DAY 56: *Depression*

"But the Holy Spirit produces this kind of fruit in our lives:
love, joy, peace, patience, kindness, goodness, faithfulness, gentleness, and self-control.
There is no law against these things!"
Galatians 5:22-23

PRAYER:

Help me, oh Lord, to realize that in the times of distress, You are there. Thank You, Lord, for Your love. You are sovereign, Lord. You are good, wise, strong, gracious, and faithful. You are my Rock, my Shepherd, my Peace. Thank You, Lord. You are truly the greatest gift of all. Amen.

AFFIRMATION:

I accept the love and support that surrounds me.

WEEK 9: *Fear*

DAY 57: *Fear*

"They were all terrified when they saw Him. But Jesus spoke to them at once. 'Don't be afraid,' He said. 'Take courage. I am here!'"
Mark 6:50

PRAYER:

Lord, help me. I am very fearful. Teach me not to worry. Remind me to not be anxious. You do not want us to be anxious about anything, but in everything, by prayer and supplication, with thanksgiving, let your request be made known to God. Lord, my request is I am worried about my circumstances. The truth is, I am fearful of the outcome. Lord, I need Your help. Amen.

AFFIRMATION:

I am strong and powerful.

DAY 58: *Fear*

"Fearing people is a dangerous trap, but trusting the Lord means safety."

Proverbs 29:25

PRAYER:

Lord, the storm keeps on raging in my life. It seems that I am being tossed and driven. My eyes will remain on you, Lord. I am fearful, but I know this storm will cease. Lord, give me Your assurance that it's going to be peace. I must say the Lord is my helper; I will not be afraid. What can man do to me? My trust is in the Lord. Amen.

AFFIRMATION:

I shall overcome every obstacle.

DAY 59: *Fear*

"So that we may boldly say, the Lord is my helper,
and I will not fear what man shall do unto me."
Hebrews 13:6

PRAYER:

Lord, today I will keep my mind on You and remain in perfect peace as I fix my thoughts on You. Lord, let Your peace rule in my life. Lord, remind me of the peace I have in You. I never need to live in fear. Lord, You have always been in control. Amen.

AFFIRMATION:

Today is a new day full of opportunities.

DAY 60: *Fear*

"And the very hairs on your head are all numbered.
So don't be afraid. You are more valuable to God than a whole flock of sparrows."
Luke 12:7

PRAYER:

Dear Lord, Thank You for all the love that surrounds me during this difficult time. I can still see Your strong hand at work. I know that You haven't given me the spirit of fear, so therefore fear has no room in my life. I cherish each day of my life knowing that it is a gift from You. With You, God, all things are possible. So, today, I choose to hold firm to Your Word that there are many positive possibilities in my life. Amen.

AFFIRMATION:
I have unlimited potential.

DAY 61: *Fear*

"Fear not; you will no longer live in shame. Don't be afraid; there is no more disgrace for you. You will no longer remember the shame of your youth and the sorrows of widowhood."
Isaiah 54:4

PRAYER:

The Lord's Prayer
Our Father, which art in heaven, hallowed be Thy name.
Thy Kingdom come, Thy will be done on earth as it is in heaven.
Give us this day our daily bread.
And forgive us our trespasses, as we forgive them that trespass against us.
But lead us not into temptation,
But deliver us from evil.
For Thine is the Kingdom, the power, and the glory,
Forever and ever.
Amen.

AFFIRMATION:

I let go of what I cannot change and focus on what I can.

____

____

____

____

____

____

____

____

____

____

DAY 62: *Fear*

"The Lord is like a father to his children, tender and compassionate to those who fear him."

Psalm 103:13

PRAYER:

Dear Lord, I will not allow the spirit of fear to get the best of me. Lord, I am asking You to break the chain of fear. The devil cannot win this battle. Lord, there is no fear in love, but perfect love casts out fear, because fear involves torment. But, he who fears has not been made perfect in love. Lord, destroy the spirit of fear that is tormenting me. Amen.

AFFIRMATION:

I have the ability to overcome fear.

DAY 63: *Fear*

"But You, oh Lord, are a shield around me; You are my glory.
The One who holds my head high. I cried out to the Lord, and He answered me from His holy mountain. I lay down and slept, yet I woke up in safety, for the Lord was watching over me. I am not afraid of ten thousand enemies who surround me on every side."
Psalm 3:3-6

PRAYER:
Dear Lord, I thank You for the courage you have given me to face the challenges that are before me. Lord, I need Your help to overcome fear and anxiety in my life. Today, I will walk in victory. I am courageous. I cast out the spirit of fear. For today is a new day. I have been set free from the bondage of fear. In God, I trust and am not afraid. Amen.

AFFIRMATION:
I am safe and in control.

WEEK 10: *Bitterness*

DAY 64: *Bitterness*

"Look after each other so that none of you fails to receive the grace of God. Watch out that no poisonous root of bitterness grows up to trouble you, corrupting many."
Hebrews 12:15

PRAYER:

Lord, I cannot hide from You. You know all things. Lord, I confess I don't want to harbor bitterness. I cry out to You for help. I have said that I have forgiven them. I really need Your help. Let my heart be pure. I release it to You, Lord. Create in me a clean heart, oh God, and renew in me a right spirit within me. Cast me not away from Thy presence; and take not Thy Holy Spirit from me. Amen.

AFFIRMATION:

I let go of the past to move forward.

DAY 65: *Bitterness*

"Get rid of all bitterness, rage, anger, harsh words,
and slander, as well as all types of evil behavior."
Ephesians 4:31

PRAYER:

Lord, I am thankful that You are working on me. I cried out to the Lord and He heard my cry. Lord, it's my desire to obey Your Word. Your Word tells me to get rid of bitterness and to forgive. Lord, I give it all to You. Lord, forgive me for the sins of anger, revenge, and bitterness. Lord, You are faithful to forgive when we ask. Thank You, Lord, for Your great love and the gift of forgiveness. Amen.

AFFIRMATION:

I forgive to set myself free.

DAY 66: *Bitterness*

"For I perceive that thou art in the gall of bitterness, and in the bond of iniquity."
Acts 8:23

PRAYER:
Dear Lord, I pray that You will teach me to be a loving, kind, and compassionate person. Jesus tells us to love God with all our heart, all our soul, and all our mind. A second is equally important: Love your neighbor as yourself. Help me, Lord, to release these toxic emotions. I desire to be kind and compassionate to others, forgiving them, just as, Christ, You forgave me. Amen.

AFFIRMATION:
I have the courage to heal and become whole again.

DAY 67: *Bitterness*

"For we know Him that hath said, 'Vengeance belongeth unto me.
I will recompense', saith the Lord. And again, the Lord shall judge His people."
Hebrews 10:30

PRAYER:

Lord Jesus, I am thankful for this day. It's a brand new day. I am so glad that You allowed me to be here. I choose to believe Your Word. "Be gentle and ready to forgive. Never hold grudges. Remember, the Lord forgave you, so you must forgive others." I am holding firm to Your Word. I will not fight those who fight against me. I know You will vindicate on my behalf. I trust You, Lord. Amen.

AFFIRMATION:

As I forgive others, I am forgiven.

DAY 68: *Bitterness*

"Each heart knows its own bitterness, and no one else can fully share its joy."

Proverbs 14:10

PRAYER:

Lord Jesus, I come to You today with a pure heart, and I ask You to hear my prayer. The roots of bitterness are like poisonous deadly infection. Lord, if there is any in me, uproot them now and take them away. Lord, I release it in Your care. I choose to let it go. To cast all my cares upon You because You care for me. Amen.

AFFIRMATION:

Forgiveness brings peace and freedom.

DAY 69: *Bitterness*

"Their talk is foul, like the stench from an open grave. Their tongues are filled with lies. Snake venom drips from their lips. Their mouths are full of cursing and bitterness."

Romans 3:13-14

PRAYER:

Lord Jesus, I thank You for the sweet Holy Spirit. The Holy Spirit is my teacher. I read the Word of God today in James 3:8, "But no one can tame the tongue. It is restless and evil, full of deadly poison. The Holy Spirit has taught me on many occasions to hold my peace. I thank You, Lord. With You all things are possible. I give You the praise. Amen.

AFFIRMATION:

I choose to forgive those who have hurt me.

DAY 70: *Bitterness*

"But if we confess our sins to Him, He is faithful and just to forgive us our sins and to cleanse us from all wickedness."
1 John 1:9

PRAYER:

Dear Jesus, I have confessed my sins to You. I know that You have heard my prayers. Lord, empower me with the grace to forgive everyone who has offended me. I have made up my mind not to be bitter again. Please deliver me from all bitterness in the name of Jesus. Thank You, Jesus, for giving me the grace to pray today and to overcome my bitterness. Amen.

AFFIRMATION:

Confessions are good for the soul.

WEEK 11: *Betrayal*

DAY 71: *Betrayal*

"My close friends detest me. Those I loved have turned against me."
Job 19:19

PRAYER:

Jesus, it's me standing in the need of a miracle. I ask You, Lord, to remove the memories of the betrayal. I refuse to entertain them. I feel so alone. Please, stir me away from wasting my time living in the past. Heal my broken heart and bind up my wounds, because You said You are always close to the brokenhearted. Amen.

AFFIRMATION:

Everything is unfolding as it is supposed to.

DAY 72: *Betrayal*

"It is not an enemy who taunts me — I could bear that. It is not my foes
who so arrogantly insult me — I could have hidden from them.
Instead, it is you - my equal, my companion and close friend."
Psalm 55:12-14

PRAYER:

Jesus, I call on You today. I need a touch from You for my heart is bleeding. I am traumatized from this event. I trust You, Lord, to give me strength. No evil weapon formed against me shall prosper, in the name of Jesus. Amen.

AFFIRMATION:

I am releasing the past right now.

DAY 73: *Betrayal*

"For the more we suffer for Christ, the more God will shower us with His comfort through Christ."

2 Corinthians 1:5

PRAYER:

Jesus, I know that You suffered and You did not sin. Lord, help me to release this anger. I am hurting from the betrayal. This pain is in my heart. Help me to forgive the person who has hurt me. Lord, I am so glad that I can talk to You right now. I turn this over to You right now. Amen.

Affirmation:

I am deserving of love.

DAY 74: *Betrayal*

"And then shall many be offended and shall betray one another and shall hate one another."
Matthew 24:10

PRAYER:

Dear Lord, You know everything about me. You know the hurt I am feeling as a result of betrayal and broken trust. Lord, I have cried until I am weak. I lift my grief, hurts, and complaints to You. I had no idea it would ever be this way. The pain and anger I am feeling is overwhelming. I choose to give all anger and pain to You, Lord, who is my Healer. Amen.

AFFIRMATION:

I'm working on me for me.

DAY 75: *Betrayal*

"Even your brothers, members of your own family, have turned against you. They plot and raise complaints against you. Do not trust them, no matter how pleasantly they speak."

Jeremiah 12:6

PRAYER:

Lord, I give my heart to You. This has not been easy. My enemies are now behind me. I am moving forward. I have given Lord Jesus my troubles. Now, they are His troubles. I am free because the Lord has set me free. Amen.

AFFIRMATION:

I am worthy of love.

DAY 76: *Betrayal*

"Even my best friend, the one I trusted completely,
the one who shared my food, has turned against me."
Psalm 41:9

PRAYER:
Lord, help me today to get over the memories and pain involved with being betrayed by someone I loved and trust. This has been very painful. Your love towards me reminds me that I am worthy of being treated with respect, love, and honor. Lord, I have to forgive the person who has betrayed me. I turn this hurt and pain over to You, Lord. Thank You for hearing my cry. Amen.

AFFIRMATION:
I will be still and know God is God.

DAY 77: *Betrayal*

"But Jesus said, 'Judas, would you betray the Son of Man with a kiss?'"
Luke 22:48

PRAYER:
Lord, I choose to spend time with You in praise and worship. Only You can redeem my pain, hurts, and sins, and restore my heart. Lord, I trust that You will work things out for my good. Through You, Lord, I am learning what true forgiveness really means. Thank You for being the perfect example. Amen.

AFFIRMATION:
I am a trustworthy person.

WEEK 12: *Lies*

DAY 78: *Lies*

"The Lord detests lying lips, but He delights in those who tell the truth."

Proverbs 12:22

PRAYER:

Lord Jesus, You have given us peace and joy. Lord, my prayer is for everyone who has a problem with lying. Today, I pray for their deliverance. Lord, You are the truth. Your Word reminds us that the truth will set you free. "When the spirit of truth comes, he will guide you into all truth." Jesus, teach us to hold onto Your teachings. Amen.

AFFIRMATION:

Let no corrupt word proceed out of your mouth.

DAY 79: *Lies*

"A faithful witness will not lie: but a false witness will utter lies."

Proverbs 14:5

PRAYER:
Dear Lord, Thank You for the many blessings You have given me. You continue to bless me over and over again. Lord, You are mighty and powerful. Help me to overcome the lies of the enemy and to seek truth. Amen.

AFFIRMATION:
I will speak the truth only.

DAY 80: *Lies*

"The godly hate lies; the wicked cause shame and disgrace."
Proverbs 13:5

PRAYER:

Dear Jesus, I ask for help for those who have lied about me to despitefully hurt me. The enemy is wicked and he's a trickster. The lies were told to destroy me, Lord. I pray that You will protect me. Lord, today I pray for my enemies. Please forgive them for the wrong that they have done. I ask for forgiveness for the lies they spread to bring me pain. Your Word says do not lie. Do not deceive one another. Amen.

AFFIRMATION:

The old man is corrupt with deceitful desires. I am a new creation in Christ.

DAY 81: *Lies*

"Ye shall not steal, neither deal falsely, neither lie one to another."

Leviticus 19:11

PRAYER:

Heavenly Father, I lift up all those who have rejected the truth of Your Word. Lord, I know that Satan is the father of lies and his plan is to mislead us down the wrong path. Lord, my prayer is that we will hold onto the true Word of God. Your Word is truth. May the truth of Your Word ring in the ears of all who are falling by the wayside. Lord, expose every lie of the enemy. Allow Your children to see You and Your ways. Amen.

AFFIRMATION:

I will tell the truth.

DAY 82: *Lies*

"Rescue me, oh Lord, from liars and from all deceitful people."
Psalm 120:2

PRAYER:

Loving Father, we are waiting patiently for You to send answers our way. Lord, our hearts are very saddened as we wait on knowing the truth. Lord, I know that You are one who knows the truth concerning my family. Lord, let the truth be known. Lord, expose the evil works of darkness and all those that are involved. Lord, bring healing and restoration to my family in Jesus' Name. Amen.

AFFIRMATION:

This is the day the Lord has made. We will rejoice and be glad in it.

DAY 83: *Lies*

"Then keep your tongue from speaking evil and your lips from telling lies!"
Psalm 34:13

PRAYER:
Dear Lord, we all know we've been dishonest, but are we currently admitting to ourselves the truth about why we lied? Lord, as we take inventory of our lives, please forgive us for lying. Lord, You want us to tell the truth. I confess that I've been wrong. I turn away from lies and ask You to forgive me. Thank You for giving me the Holy Spirit who will guide me into all truth. Amen.

AFFIRMATION:
I enjoy telling the truth.

DAY 84: *Lies*

"God blesses you when people mock you and persecute you and lie about you and say all sorts of evil things against you because you are my followers."
Matthew 5:11

PRAYER:
Almighty God, I thank You for being our Deliverer. God forbids us from lying. Lord, I know that lying is a detrimental habit that ruins people's reputation. Your Word reminds us that "a false witness will not go unpunished, and he who speaks lies shall perish". Lord, help us to be truthful in our daily walk with You. Lord, help us to keep Your statutes and commandments. Amen.

AFFIRMATION:
I am brave enough to be honest.

WEEK 13: *Worry*

DAY 85: *Worry*

"So don't worry about tomorrow, for tomorrow will
bring its own worries. Today's trouble is enough for today."
Matthew 6:34

PRAYER:

Dear Lord, please hear my prayer. I seem to worry about everything. I ask for Your forgiveness for that. Help me to put You first in every area of my life. Help me to live one day at a time. Lord, help me to focus on what You are doing for me right now. Help me not to worry about tomorrow. Help me to trust You more and worry less. In Jesus' Name. Amen.

AFFIRMATION:

I am healing and strengthening every day.

DAY 86: *Worry*

"Worry weighs a person down; an encouraging word cheers a person up."

Proverbs 12:25

PRAYER:

Lord, when troubles occur in our lives, it's easy to worry. I say that I am not going to worry. Lord, I find myself worrying rather than trusting that You will work it out. Lead me with Your spirit to focus on positive things. Lord, somehow I know that You will calm the storm. Touch me with Your peace and help my disturbed mind know that with You, I need not to worry. Amen.

AFFIRMATION:

Happiness is a choice, and today I choose to be happy.

DAY 87: *Worry*

"Give all your worries and cares to God, for He cares about You."

1 Peter 5:7

PRAYER:

Dear Lord, I'm worried and full of fear. Lord, I need answers. I have so many questions and concerns. Today, I feel lost and overwhelmed. Lord, You know that my heart is heavy. The world seems out of control, full of evil. During tough times, give me the confidence to trust You. Amen.

AFFIRMATION:

Everything I need is within me right now.

DAY 88: *Worry*

"But when I am afraid, I will put my trust in You."

Psalm 56:3

PRAYER:

Lord, I need Your help. Keep me calm and focused on what I can change. Lord, help me to fix my thoughts on You, and fill my heart with peace. Lord, it is hard to keep going on not knowing where my child is. God, You know all things. Please protect my child wherever he is. May I trust in You to see me through. You are all I need. Amen.

AFFIRMATION:

Today is a phenomenal day.

DAY 89: *Worry*

"And if God cares so wonderfully for flowers that are here today and thrown into the fire tomorrow, He will certainly care for you. Why do you have so little faith? And don't be concerned about what to eat and what to drink. Don't worry about such things. These things dominate the thoughts of unbelievers all over the world, but your Father already knows your needs."

Luke 12:28-30

PRAYER:

Dear Jesus, I am reminded that You do not want me to worry. Too many things occupy my mind. Let me trust in Your will alone. I can do all things through Christ. Lord, help me to take one day at a time. Amen.

AFFIRMATION:

Today is filled with possibility.

DAY 90: *Worry*

"Can all your worries add a single moment to your life? And if worry can't accomplish a little thing like that, what's the use of worrying over bigger things?"

Luke 12:25-26

PRAYER:

Lord Jesus, thank You for Your grace and mercy. Lord, You give me new mercy every day. Lord, I thank You for Your loving kindness. Lord, I trust in Your will alone. Your Word tells me where there is love, there is no fear. Help me to live gratefully with dependence on You, trusting You to take care of my loved one. Amen.

AFFIRMATION:

I am strong enough to overcome challenges.

DAY 91: *Worry*

"When doubts filled my mind, your comfort gave me renewed hope and cheer."
Psalm 94:19

PRAYER:
Lord, I thank You for being my strength and my God in whom I trust. You are the strength of my life; You are my rock, my fortress, and my protector. Lord, I'm casting all my cares on You, because I know You care for me. I choose not to worry today. Lord, I trust You will calm the storm. Amen.

AFFIRMATION:
Today, I choose only happiness and joy.

WEEK 14: *Anger*

DAY 92: *Anger*

"And don't sin by letting anger control you. Don't let the sun go down while you are still angry, for anger gives a foothold to the devil. Amen."
Ephesians 4:26-27

PRAYER:

Dear Lord, today I come before You as I am experiencing anger. I ask You to bless me with perfect peace. Lord, You are my peace. I pray that my anger would subside. My desire is to worship and praise You. Fill my heart with compassion. Lord, You are the Prince of Peace. I will praise You, Lord. Amen.

AFFIRMATION:

I dedicate my life to peace and harmony.

DAY 93: *Anger*

"Understand this, my dear brothers and sisters: You must all be quick to listen, slow to speak, and slow to get angry. Human anger does not produce the righteousness God desires."

James 1:19-20

PRAYER:

Dear Jesus, please ease my anger, pain, and heartache, and let me feel love and happiness. You are the One who binds up and heals the broken-hearted. I receive my healing by faith, and I thank You for giving me the grace to stand firm until the process is complete. Thank You, Lord, that You watch over Your Word to perform it. Amen.

AFFIRMATION:

I am free of anger, hatred, and discontent.

DAY 94: *Anger*

"Control your temper, for anger labels you a fool."
Ecclesiastes 7:9

PRAYER:

Dear Lord, bring peace to my mind and my heart as I feel angry about this current storm. Calm the storm, Lord. May I take hold of Your promise that You will never leave me nor forsake me. Lord, I ask You to fight my battles. Give me Your peace, Lord. May it rule over my life. In Jesus' Name, I pray. Amen.

AFFIRMATION:

I now choose to stay calm in difficult or frustrating situations.

DAY 95: *Anger*

"Stop being angry! Turn from your rage! Do not lose your temper – it only leads to harm. For the wicked will be destroyed, but those who trust in the Lord will possess the land."

Psalm 3:8-9

PRAYER:

Lord, help me turn from anger and irritation and pursue peace and harmony. Protect me that I will not sin against You. I pray that I will overcome anger. Lord, Your Word reminds me not to be overcome by evil, but overcome evil with good. Please alleviate my suffering and grant me peace of mind. Amen.

AFFIRMATION:

I attract peace and harmony in all situations in my life.

DAY 96: *Anger*

"Oh Lord, don't rebuke me in Your anger or discipline me in Your rage."

Psalm 6:1

PRAYER:

Lord, may the words of my mouth and meditation of my heart be acceptable in Your sight. Lord, let my love reflect Your character. Lord, give me the wisdom to know what to say and when to say it. Lord, I thank You for Your love and understanding, and I put my trust in You right now. I praise You for Your goodness. Amen.

AFFIRMATION:

I clear and release any and all ways I am holding onto anger!

DAY 97: *Anger*

"He that hath knowledge spareth his words:
and a man of understanding is of an excellent spirit."
Proverbs 17:27

PRAYER:

Dear Lord, thank You for being an anchor for me today. I give my worries over to You, as I know You will work all things together for the good of those who love You and are called according to Your purpose. Lord, my child is out there somewhere. I don't know where he is. I am a concerned mother. My heart is troubled. Lord, I don't want to be angry. Give me Your peace, Lord. May it rule over my life. Through Jesus Christ, Amen.

AFFIRMATION:

I choose to reclaim my peace.

DAY 98: *Anger*

"The Lord is merciful and compassionate, slow to get angry and filled with unfailing love."
Psalm 145:8

PRAYER:

Jesus, I call on You today. I have a son who is missing. Each day, I wait to hear his voice. I haven't heard from him. Lord, my heart is crushed. I am upset. I don't know where he is. Lord, please answer my prayer. Lord, where is my son? Lord, this battle is too big for me. Lord, this battle belongs to You. I give it to You right now. I pray that all unrighteous anger flees from me. By Your Spirit, I declare rest and peace in my life. In Jesus' Name, I pray. Amen.

AFFIRMATION:

I let go of anger and embrace gentleness.

WEEK 15: *Darkness*

DAY 99: *Darkness*

"For thou art my lamp, oh Lord, and the Lord will lighten my darkness."
2 Samuel 22:29

PRAYER:

Dear Lord, You are the keeper of my soul. Lord, I feel like I am in a dark and gloomy place right now. I feel tired and overwhelmed as if I'm shutting down. Today, my heart seems heavy, and I would like to know where my child is. Lord, You know every circumstance or situation I am facing. I cling to You with hope, faith, and assurance that You will pull me out of this dark place. Thank You for coming to see about me. Amen.

AFFIRMATION:

This too shall pass.

DAY 100: *Darkness*

"When I looked for good, then evil came unto me;
and when I waited for light, there came darkness."
Job 30:26

PRAYER:
Dear Lord, this has been the darkest hour of my life. I need you, Lord, to be my strength. I am weak and lonely. My heart cries out to You. I need a touch from You, Lord. I desperately need to be in Your presence. Darkness is all around me in this evil world. Give me the courage to face one day at a time. In Jesus' Name, Amen.

AFFIRMATION:
I will remain calm even during this difficult situation.

DAY 101: *Darkness*

"Do not gloat over me, my enemies! For though I fall, I will rise again. Though I sit in darkness, the Lord will be my light."

Micah 7:9

PRAYER:

Dear Lord, I'm not at a good place within myself. My back is against the wall. The waters are deep. I am drowning from my teardrops. I call on You to rescue me from this dark pit. I never knew that I would have to go through this. I pray that You would send someone to help bear my burden. Please guide me out of this pit. Amen.

AFFIRMATION:

I have the ability to recover from difficulties.

DAY 102: *Darkness*

"My eyes are blinded by my tears. Each day,
I beg for Your help, oh Lord; I lift my hands to You for mercy."
Psalm 88:9

PRAYER:

Dear Lord, I thank You for being the light of this world. Help me to walk in Your light. Lord, please turn my darkness into light. Teach me to rejoice when things become difficult. Jesus, I put all of my trust in You. Amen.

AFFIRMATION:

I will allow my light to shine, and the darkness will disappear.

DAY 103: *Darkness*

"Jesus spoke to the people once more and said, 'I am the light of the world. If you follow Me, you won't have to walk in darkness, because you will have the light that leads to life.'"
John 8:12

PRAYER:

Lord, please heal my wounds. My heart is broken. My heart is hurting. My loved one has not been found. I have cried, and I am weak. Touch my heart this day. I pray to You as I am desperate for help. Lord, help me to "be still" and know that You are God. Lord, You are my healer and my peace. Amen.

AFFIRMATION:

I choose to find light within the darkness.

DAY 104: *Darkness*

"I create the light and make the darkness. I send good times and bad times. I, the Lord, am the one who does these things. Open up, oh heavens, and pour out your righteousness. Let the earth open wide so salvation and righteousness can sprout up together. I, the Lord, created them."

Isaiah 45:7-8

PRAYER:

Lord, You are a merciful God when everything seems to be going wrong. I am in a dark season. Even darkness has a deadline. Lord, I don't have the answers. I am in distress, and I am calling upon You for answers. Please rescue me. You are a present help at all times. Amen.

AFFIRMATION:

Nothing stays the same. Even the darkest night will end.

DAY 105: *Darkness*

"For we wrestle not against flesh and blood, but against principalities, against powers, against the rulers of the darkness of this world, against spiritual wickedness in high places."

Ephesians 6:12

PRAYER:

My God, it seems like my world is crumbling around me. The storms are raging in my life. Remind me, Lord, that You are always with me. You will never leave or forsake me. Lord, help me to rely on You. Your Word is a lamp for my feet, a light on my path. I will trust You, Lord. Amen.

AFFIRMATION:

I walk in the light.

WEEK 16: *Shame*

DAY 106: *Shame*

"Because the Sovereign Lord helped me, I will not be disgraced. Therefore, I have set my face like a stone, determined to do His will. And I know that I will not be put to shame."

Isaiah 50:7

PRAYER:

Lord, I want to thank You for Your love and kindness and making it possible for me to see today. I will lift Your holy name and praise You, in the name of Jesus.

AFFIRMATION:

I will no longer allow myself to be a victim of shame.

DAY 107: *Shame*

"Oh my God, I trust in Thee; let me not be ashamed, let not mine enemies triumph over me."
Psalm 25:2

PRAYER:

Father, I rebuke every spirit of shame. The spirit of shame has no rule over my life. Let Your angels guard me against every incursion of the spirit of shame, in the name of Jesus.

AFFIRMATION:

I am capable of change.

DAY 108: *Shame*

"I cling to Your laws. Lord, don't let me be put to shame!"
Psalm 119:31

PRAYER:
Father, arise and fight for me. You know all that are pointing their finger at me, those fighting me with shame. Lord, You, my Banner, arise and fight those who are fighting me, in Jesus' Name.

AFFIRMATION:
I refuse to be controlled by guilt and shame.

DAY 109: *Shame*

"Those who hate you will be clothed in shame, and the tents of the wicked will be no more."

Job 8:22

PRAYER:

Dear Lord, by the power, bring me out of every pit of shame and disgrace the enemy has put me into. Lord, You are my Deliverer, and I trust You. Amen.

AFFIRMATION:

On this journey, shame cannot control me anymore.

DAY 110: *Shame*

"In You, Lord, I have taken refuge;
let me never be put to shame; deliver me in Your righteousness."
Psalm 31:1

PRAYER:
Lord, I thank You for bringing people into my life that love and encourage me on this journey. It is only in You, Lord Jesus, that we now find hope to deal with what we are going through. I refuse to walk in shame. God's truth will be revealed to me.

AFFIRMATION:
I declare that the Lord is my Guide, my Deliverer, my Comforter, and I will not walk in shame.

DAY 111: *Shame*

"Instead of shame and dishonor, you will enjoy a double share of honor. You will possess a double portion of prosperity in your land, and everlasting joy will be yours."
Isaiah 61:7

PRAYER:
Lord, I thank You for this day. I come before You today seeking Your face and asking for answers. Lord, I believe Your Word. Let every ounce of shame be removed in the name of Jesus, Amen.

AFFIRMATION:
All things are working for my good.

DAY 112: *Shame*

"Looking unto Jesus, the Author and Finisher of our faith;
who for the joy that was set before Him, endured the cross, despising
the shame, and is set down at the right hand of the throne of God."
Hebrews 12:12

PRAYER:
Lord, I will give You praise. I have been redeemed to show forth the glory of the Lord. Amen.

AFFIRMATION:
Every experience that I have gone through has helped me to help others.

WEEK 17: *Despair*

DAY 113: *Despair*

"Lord, You know the hopes of the helpless. Surely, You will hear their cries and comfort them. You will bring justice to the orphans and the oppressed, so mere people can no longer terrify them."

Psalm 10:17-18

PRAYER:

Dear Lord, You are our ever-present help in times of trouble. You are the answer that I need. Thank You that You have promised to be with me, even when I am in deep despair. I am thankful that You always help me. Amen.

AFFIRMATION:

I choose to focus on positive thoughts and feelings.

DAY 114: *Despair*

"I have told you all this so that you may have peace in Me. Here on earth you will have many trials and sorrows. But take heart, because I have overcome the world."
John 16:33

PRAYER:

Dear Lord, today, let me experience Your holy comforting presence. I don't want to give up. I am trying my best to keep pushing and moving forward. Amen.

AFFIRMATION:

I am loved and appreciated by those around me.

DAY 115: *Despair*

"From the depths of despair, oh Lord, I call for Your help. Hear my cry, oh Lord. Pay attention to my prayer."
Psalm 130:1-2

PRAYER:
Dear Lord, I am calling on You today. I call upon You during this time of hopelessness. Be my hope, Lord. You know exactly what I am going through. Lord, I ask You to comfort me during this difficult time. Amen.

AFFIRMATION:
I am letting go of my stress.

DAY 116: *Despair*

"Why am I discouraged? Why is my heart so sad? I will put my hope in God! I will praise Him again - my Savior and my God."
Psalm 43:5

PRAYER:

Dear Lord, In times of despair, I need to draw closer to You. Help me to remember that suffering in this world produces patience and perseverance. Help me to look to Jesus as the anchor of my soul.

AFFIRMATION:

I am surrounded by love and support.

DAY 117: *Despair*

"But in my distress, I cried out to the Lord; yes, I prayed to my God for help. He heard me from His sanctuary; my cry to Him reached His ears."

Psalm 18:6

PRAYER:

Dear Lord, I feel all alone right now. I know that Your Word declares that You are with me always. Please comfort me during this difficult time. Pour out Your love and compassion. I'm desperately in need of it, Lord. Amen.

AFFIRMATION:

I'm getting stronger every day.

DAY 118: *Despair*

"From the end of the earth will I cry unto Thee, when my heart is overwhelmed; lead me to the rock that is higher than I."
Psalm 61:2

PRAYER:
Dear Lord, I thank You for this day. I bow down before You as my only source of hope. My spirit is weak. I need You to renew my strength and let me soar high like an eagle during these moments of despair. Your grace is sufficient, Lord. Be my light, Lord. My faith is in You. Amen.

AFFIRMATION:
I'm grateful for my inner strength and resilience.

DAY 119: *Despair*

"To all who mourn in Israel, He will give a crown of beauty for ashes, a joyous blessing instead of mourning, festive praise instead of despair. In their righteousness, they will be like great oaks that the Lord has planted for His great glory."

Isaiah 61:3

PRAYER:

Dear Lord, I ask You to please help me. I desperately need Your help. I am in deep despair. I lift up my hands to You in prayer. Provide the grace, strength, and faith I need to take the step to reach my destination. Lord, guide me that I may walk and not faint. Amen.

AFFIRMATION:

I'm thriving. I'm becoming the best version of myself.

WEEK 18: *Emotions*

DAY 120: *Emotions*

"Oh Lord, if You heal me, I will be truly healed.
If You save me, I will be truly saved. My praises are for You alone!"
Jeremiah 17:14

PRAYER:

Oh Lord, hear my cry today. I need You to soothe me with Your love. Lord, You know everyone who is in need of emotional healing and the hurt and pain they are going through. I ask You to meet each one at their own point of need. May they find love and comfort in You, Lord. Amen.

AFFIRMATION:

I will open up myself to experience the healing power of Jesus Christ.

DAY 121: *Emotions*

"Even when I walk through the darkest valley, I will not be afraid,
for You are close beside me. Your rod and Your staff protect me and comfort me."
Psalm 23:4

PRAYER:

Dear Lord, Give me the strength to move forward on the path you've laid out for me. As I go through the trials of life, help me to realize that you are with me at all times and in all things. For You are the Lord who heals. Amen.

AFFIRMATION:

I choose to release fear. I will not entertain hopeless thoughts.

DAY 122: *Emotions*

"He will wipe every tear from their eyes, and there will be no more death or sorrow or crying or pain. All these things are gone forever."
Revelation 21:4

PRAYER:
Dear Jesus, Thank You because You are the Giver of peace. My heart is troubled and is in need of Your peace right now. Lord, guard my heart, heal me emotionally, and keep my mind fixed on You. Thank You, Lord, as I wait patiently on You. Amen.

AFFIRMATION:
I value my emotions and my life.

DAY 123: *Emotions*

"Lord, Your discipline is good, for it leads to life
and health. You restore my health and allow me to live!"
Isaiah 38:16

PRAYER:

Dear Lord, many of us need healing. Help me to receive my healing so that I may be whole and that I may be able to then minister to others in a way that brings You fullness of glory. Lord, I believe that You are my Healer and Redeemer. Amen.

AFFIRMATION:

I will soak in God's peace, today.

DAY 124: *Emotions*

"I am leaving you with a gift - peace of mind and heart. And the peace I give is a gift the world cannot give. So don't be troubled or afraid."

John 14:27

PRAYER:

Lord, I am hurting, wounded, betrayed, and brokenhearted. My hope is for me to recover from the deep hurt I feel inside. Help me to let go of this pain. Thank You for Your healing power. Amen.

AFFIRMATION:

I surround myself with happier thoughts.

DAY 125: *Emotions*

"Remember Your promise to me; it is my only hope.
Your promise revives me; it comforts me in all my troubles."
Psalm 119: 49-50

PRAYER:

Lord, I admit at times I allow my mind to wonder and I seem to think the worst. I don't wanna do that any longer. Lord, I want to walk in freedom. Today, I forgive all who have hurt me. I choose to forgive them. Give me the faith to walk in freedom and victory. In Jesus' Name, Amen.

AFFIRMATION:

Today, I am working towards being happier.

DAY 126: *Emotions*

"When you go through deep waters, I will be with you. When you go through rivers of difficulty, you will not drown. When you walk through the fire of oppression, you will not be burned up; the flames will not consume you."

Isaiah 43:2

PRAYER:

Dear Lord, please restore me. I pray You lay Your healing hands on me for the emotional pain that I am dealing with. Lord, only You can release the anguish I feel within me. Fill me with peace and joy I know can only come from You during this hard time. Lord, walk closely beside me during my journey to healing.

AFFIRMATION:

Today, I will gain emotional strength.

WEEK 19: *Never Give Up*

DAY 127: *Never Give Up*

"Work willingly at whatever you do, as though you were working for the Lord rather than for people. Remember that the Lord will give you an inheritance as your reward and that the Master you are serving is Christ."

Colossians 3:23-24

PRAYER:

Dear Jesus, I am sharing my heart with You, today. Don't let me give up on life or whatever God asked me to do. Help me not to get tired of doing good. Don't let me get discouraged and give up. I am holding onto the promise. I will not be discouraged. I will reap a harvest of blessings at the appropriate time. Amen.

AFFIRMATION:

I set my heart towards possibilities.

DAY 128: *Never Give Up*

"Jesus looked at them intently and said, 'Humanly speaking, it is impossible, but, with God, everything is possible.'"
Matthew 19:26

PRAYER:

Dear Lord, I need You each and every day of my life. I will never give up. My hope is in You. I believe that You are with me always. Help me to trust in Your goodness and to find hope in Your promises. Keep me grounded in Your love and help me to never give up. In Jesus' Name, Amen.

AFFIRMATION:

I am not giving up. I'm awake and motivated.

DAY 129: *Never Give Up*

"You will show me the way of life, granting me the joy of Your presence and the pleasures of living with You forever."
Psalm 16:11

PRAYER:

Dear Lord, guide me and lead me through every trial I face. Help me draw my strength from You. I am more than a conqueror. You are my protector, Lord. Give me strength, faith, and hope, and, most of all, give me guidance each and every day. I ask You to give me strength to carry on. In Jesus' Name, Amen.

AFFIRMATION:

I am strong enough to get through this.

DAY 130: *Never Give Up*

"Always be joyful. Never stop praying. Be thankful in all circumstances, for this is God's will for you who belong to Christ Jesus."
1 Thessalonians 5:16-18

PRAYER:

Dear Lord, I thank You for this day. Help me to overcome my fears and worries. I need Your strength now. I am weary and tired. Grant me the grace to keep going on. Please fill my heart with Your love and remind me of my purpose. Amen.

AFFIRMATION:

I choose to be zealous and passionate.

DAY 131: *Never Give Up*

"God blesses those who patiently endure testing and temptation. Afterward, they will receive the crown of Life that God has promised to those who love Him."

James 1:12

PRAYER:

My God, You are faithful and just in all that You do. Your Word is true. Your work is trustworthy. Your wisdom helps us better understand ourselves and others. I trust You for help and strength to pass every test. Help me to submit to Your guidance wholeheartedly, that I may keep pursuing the path You have for my life. Amen.

AFFIRMATION:

In tough times, I persevere.

DAY 132: *Never Give Up*

"So, let's not get tired of doing what is good. At just the right time, we will reap a harvest of blessing if we don't give up."
Galatians 6:9

PRAYER:

Dear Lord, I am going through a very difficult time. You are my hope and will never leave me or forsake me. Despite all that I am going through, I will not give up. Give me the strength and courage to persevere. In Jesus' Name, I pray. Amen.

AFFIRMATION:

I will never give up. I will never lose hope.

Day 133: *Never Give Up*

"He gives power to the weak and strength to the powerless.
Even youths will become tired and young men will fall in exhaustion,
but those who trust in the Lord will find new strength. They will soar high on
wings like eagles. They will run and not grow weary. They will walk and not faint."
Isaiah 40:29-31

PRAYER:

Dear Lord, You alone know the sorry deep within my heart. Thank you that when I am weak, You are strong. Lord, don't let me give up. Give me a measure of Your strength so that I might not give into discouragement. I can do all things through Jesus Christ. Amen.

AFFIRMATION:

I see my strengths and will use them wisely.

WEEK 20: *Tears*

DAY 134: *Tears*

"But in my distress, I cried out to the Lord; yes, I prayed to my God for help. He heard from His sanctuary; my cry to Him reached His ears."

Psalm 18:6

PRAYER:

Lord, You are Jehovah Rapha, my Healer. I pray for Your healing power to be extended to me, Your child. I pour my heart out to You. Lord, I ask that You heal me. Lord, You are able to restore me.

AFFIRMATION:

My strength is greater than any struggle.

DAY 135: *Tears*

"You keep track of all my sorrows. You have collected all my tears in Your bottle. You have recorded each one in Your book. My enemies will retreat when I call to You for help. This I know: God is on my side!"
Psalm 56:8-9

PRAYER:
Lord, my tears are speaking out for me. Emotionally, I am a mess right now, and I cannot seem to be able to get a handle on how to find my way out of my distress. Lord, I need You to heal me. My heart is broken, and I need You to help right now. Amen.

AFFIRMATION:
I focus on what I can control and let go of what I cannot.

DAY 136: *Tears*

"For the Lamb on the throne will be their shepherd. He will lead them to springs of life-giving water. And God will wipe every tear from their eyes."

Revelation 7:17

PRAYER:

Dear Lord, I am here before You as Your broken-hearted child. Lord, You have seen my tears. The emotional grief I have been dealing with has become more than I can bear on my own. Please come and intervene in my life, and help me overcome my sorrow. Lord, I am ready to walk this path to emotional healing. Amen.

AFFIRMATION:

I am getting better.

DAY 137: *Tears*

"I am worn out from sobbing. All night, I flood
my bed with weeping, drenching it with my tears."
Psalm 6:6

PRAYER:

Lord, You are faithful. I am going through one of the greatest emotional upheavals of my life. I need You more than ever to help me get through. Lord, I need answers, and I wait on You. Please bring beauty from my ashes. Amen.

AFFIRMATION:

I am healing, and I will be at peace.

DAY 138: *Tears*

"My friends scorn me, but I pour out my tears to God. I need someone to mediate between God and me, as a person mediates between friends."
Job 16:20-21

PRAYER:
Lord Jesus, I feel as though I am in a battle for my sanity right now. I realize that the real source of my problem is the pain I am struggling with. My pain has taken me to a hard emotional place in my mind. Lord, I need You to renew a right spirit within me.

AFFIRMATION:
Without hesitation, I leap forward.

DAY 139: *Tears*

"Cry aloud before the Lord, oh walls of beautiful Jerusalem! Let your tears flow like a river day and night. Give yourselves no rest; give your eyes no relief."
Lamentation 2:18

PRAYER:
Dear Lord, when fear comes against me and threatens to end my hope, my heart will not be discouraged. I remain confident of this: I will see your goodness and your glory in my life. Guide my path so that no matter what it leads me closer to You. Amen.

AFFIRMATION:
My spirit is renewed.

DAY 140: *Tears*

"Those who plant in tears will harvest with shouts of joy."
Psalm 126:5

PRAYER:
Dear Jesus, thank You for Your promise to be our refuge in times of trouble. I am under a great deal of emotional burden and pain, and I can't find a way to rise above the pain. I am pouring out my heart before You, seeking Your help and healing. I pray that You heal my pain and return joyful thoughts to my mind."

AFFIRMATION:
I take captive any negative thoughts and memories. They have no place in my heart or mind.

WEEK 21: *Early in the Morning*

DAY 141: *Early in the Morning*

"The Sovereign Lord has given me His words of wisdom so that I know how to comfort the weary. Morning by morning, He awakens me and opens my understanding to His will."

Isaiah 50:4

PRAYER:

Dear Lord, Today is a new day. I ask You to help me. Everywhere I walk, let it be Your path. Everything I see, let it be through Your eyes. For what I am going through now, let me place it in Your hands. For I know You care for me. I thank you that You promise to be with me always. In Your name, I pray. Amen.

AFFIRMATION:

I woke up this morning with a smile. It's a beautiful day. I'm glad to be a part of it.

DAY 142: *Early in the Morning*

"The faithful love of the Lord never ends. His mercies never cease.
Great is His faithfulness; His mercies begin afresh each morning."
Lamentations 3:22-23

PRAYER:

Good morning, Jesus. You came to bring us life and life more abundantly. You gave us hope. We now have access to heaven and the limitless goodness and wisdom of the Father. We believe that You are making all things new. We are ready for a fresh start. Thank you, Lord Jesus, for helping us in troubled times. Amen.

AFFIRMATION:

Today we welcome a peaceful and gentle day. We are worthy of today.

DAY 143: *Early in the Morning*

"Satisfy us each morning with Your unfailing love,
so we may sing for joy to the end of our lives."
Psalm 90:14

PRAYER:

Dear Lord, great is Your love towards me. Let nothing separate me from You today. Lord, help me to spread love everywhere I go. Thank You that You are greater than anything we may face in our day. I am mindful that Your presence goes with me everywhere. I ask that Your grace covers me, Amen.

AFFIRMATION:

I am open to love and healing.

DAY 144: *Early in the Morning*

"Let me hear of your unfailing love each morning, for I am trusting You. Show me where to walk, for I give myself to You."
Psalm 143:8

PRAYER:
Dear Lord, You are my shield and strong Tower. Help me to anchor myself to You today. Teach me how to stand strong in You. Thank You, Lord, that You love me and nothing can ever take that away from me. May I live a life of true love as I see You at work around me today. In Jesus' Name, Amen.

AFFIRMATION:
I can do all things in love.

DAY 145: *Early in the Morning*

"Listen to my voice in the morning, Lord. Each morning I bring my requests to You and wait expectantly."
Psalm 5:3

PRAYER:

Lord, I need to hear from You. I have commanded my morning. Today, I make the commitment to start having a daily quiet time. I have so many concerns and cares, and they weigh me down. I need Your guidance, Lord. I will follow You, Lord, and wait on You. Amen.

AFFIRMATION:

Today I will choose kindness and love.

DAY 146: *Early in the Morning*

"My soul waiteth for the Lord more than they that watch for the morning: I say, more than they that watch for the morning."
Psalm 130:6

PRAYER:

Good morning, Lord. Thank You for a new day. Thank You that Your compassion is renewed every morning. Great is Your faithfulness and Your steadfast love, oh Lord! Please go before me today. Give me strength in the midst of any frustrations or hurts. I surrender this day to You, trusting in Your mercy, strength, and grace. In Jesus' Name, Amen.

AFFIRMATION:

Today, I can make a difference.

DAY 147: *Early in the Morning*

"But as for me, I will sing about Your power. Each morning I will sing with joy about Your unfailing love. For you have been my refuge, a place of safety when I am in distress."
Psalm 59:16

PRAYER:

Dear Lord, I thank You for the complete joy I have in You. I praise You for turning my wailing into dancing. Thank You for removing shame and mourning and for clothing me with your joy. You promise me joy in the morning. Lord Jesus, I receive joy this morning. Amen.

AFFIRMATION:

My day begins and ends with gratitude and joy.

WEEK 22: *Pressing On*

DAY 148: *Pressing On*

"Let us hold tightly without wavering to the hope
we affirm, for God can be trusted to keep His promise."
Hebrews 10:23

PRAYER:

God, help me accept the things I can't change, give me the courage to change the things I can, and give me the wisdom to know the difference. Please God, help me have the wisdom that I need to apply to my life daily. I'm needing some comfort right now. May your peace guide my heart and mind in Jesus' Name, Amen.

AFFIRMATION:

I am victorious. I cannot be defeated. Jesus is with me always.

DAY 149: *Pressing On*

"I don't mean to say that I have already achieved these things or that I have already reached perfection. But I press on to possess that perfection for which Christ Jesus first possessed me. No, dear brothers and sisters, I have not achieved it, but I focus on this one thing: Forgetting the past and looking forward to what lies ahead, I press on to reach the end of the race and receive the heavenly prize for which God, through Christ Jesus, is calling us."

Philippians 3:12-14

PRAYER:

Dear Lord, Thank You for the strength to press forward, that You are a God of love and forgiveness, that You don't want us to give up. I'm determined to press on. Lord, You are my strength. I thank You for being there for me, in Jesus' Name, Amen.

AFFIRMATION:

I will press on. I am unstoppable.

DAY 150: *Pressing On*

"I fight the good fight for the true faith. Hold tightly to the eternal life to which God has called you, which you have declared so well before many witnesses."
1 Timothy 6:12

PRAYER:
Dear Lord, Thank You for the precious gift of life. You allowed me to see this day, and I'm grateful. I will continue to press to finish what you started in me. I'm in a storm. Lord, this storm will cease. I trust You, Lord, that You will get me through this difficult time. Thank You, Lord, that You are the author of my life, and You can turn my salvation around. I give You praise for doing it in Jesus' Name, Amen.

AFFIRMATION:
Greater is he that is in me than he that is in the world. I will press on and never give up.

____

____

____

____

____

____

____

____

____

____

____

____

____

DAY 151: *Pressing On*

"We are pressed on every side by troubles, but we are not crushed.
We are perplexed, but not driven to despair. We are hunted down,
but never abandoned by God. We got knocked down, but we are not destroyed."
2 Corinthians 4:8-9

PRAYER:

Dear Lord, thank You for new mercies every day. Your grace is sufficient unto me. Lord, You will never abandon Your children. I'm more determined to press on. I know that things will get better for me. I put my trust in You, Lord. You will see me through this difficult time. Lord, You are the source of my strength and my great comforter. Amen.

AFFIRMATION:

The Lord goes before me and prepares the way ahead. I will press on and follow the Lord.

DAY 152: *Pressing On*

"Now all glory to God, who is able, through His mighty power at work within us, to accomplish infinitely more than we might ask or think. Glory to Him in the church and in Christ Jesus through all generations forever and ever. Amen."

Ephesians 3:20-21

PRAYER:

Oh Lord, I am weary and tired. I have been trying to weather the storm. I need Your power and strength to deal with this storm. Help me learn to patiently endure the hard times and honor You in the midst of them as I walk by faith. I will continue to press on with my walk with the Lord. Thank You, Lord, for strength to endure as a strong soldier. Amen.

AFFIRMATION:

I will run the race that is set before me. There is another press on the inside of me.

DAY 153: *Pressing On*

"Dear brothers and sisters, when troubles of any kind come your way, consider it an opportunity for great joy. For you know that when your faith is tested, your endurance has a chance to grow. So let it grow, for when your endurance is fully developed, you will be perfect and complete, needing nothing."

James 1:2-4

PRAYER:

Dear Lord, we thank You. For the things we see now will soon be gone, but the things we cannot see will last forever. For our present troubles are small and won't last very long. So we don't look at the troubles we can see now, rather, we fix our gaze on things that cannot be seen. Be our comforter, our healer, and bring us peace. In Jesus' Name, Amen.

AFFIRMATION:

No weapon formed against me shall prosper.

DAY 154: *Pressing On*

"Therefore, since we are surrounded by such a huge crowd of witnesses to the life of faith, let us strip off every weight that slows us down, especially the sin that so easily trips us up. And let us run with endurance the race God has set before us. We do this by keeping our eyes on Jesus, the champion who initiates and perfects our faith. Because of the joy awaiting Him, He endured the cross, disregarding its shame. Now He is seated in the place of honor beside God's throne."

Hebrews 12:1-2

PRAYER:

Lord, the weight that's on my shoulders is very heavy. Lord, I need You now more than ever. Help me recognize and accept Your divine help. Lord, I will trust in You at all times. I will remain steadfast in the faith and trust God always. In Jesus' Name, Amen.

AFFIRMATION:

Everything is working for my good today.

WEEK 23: *Understanding*

DAY 155: *Understanding*

"Wisdom is the principal thing; therefore get wisdom:
And with all thy getting, get understanding."
Proverbs 4:7

PRAYER:
Dear Lord, I pray that You will give me the spirit of wisdom and revelation, so that I may know You better. Help me to walk the path that You have for me. Let me act out love and spread kindness among others. In Jesus' Name, Amen.

AFFIRMATION:
Being kind is the hallmark of practicing patience and understanding.

DAY 156: *Understanding*

"But true wisdom and power are found in God;; counsel and understanding are His."
Job 12:13

PRAYER:

Dear Lord Jesus, help me to treat each person I encounter as You would, with respect and love, forgiving others and asking for forgiveness myself when needed. Grant me wisdom and understanding. Help me to remember that You love me. Remind me that I am Your child and Your representative to the world around me. I desire to have an understanding of what You are requiring of me. In Jesus' Name, Amen.

AFFIRMATION:

I increase in wisdom, knowledge, and understanding daily.

DAY 157: *Understanding*

"For the Lord grants wisdom! From His mouth comes knowledge and understanding."

Proverbs 2:6

PRAYER:

Dear Lord Jesus, I ask that You please fill my heart with patience, kindness, and grant me understanding. I need this in all my dealings while facing various challenges and difficulties. Lord, bless me with the gift of understanding. In Jesus' Name, Amen.

AFFIRMATION:

I am a well-spring of wisdom and understanding.

DAY 158: *Understanding*

"And the Spirit of the Lord will rest on him. The spirit of wisdom and understanding, the spirit of counsel and might, the spirit of knowledge and the fear of the Lord."

Isaiah 11:2

PRAYER:

Dear Jesus, grant me the gift of understanding. Help me, Lord, to always see You at work and in the lives of others. Bless me with understanding and insight. Help me to understand. Widen my vision beyond my own small world to embrace knowledge and love for others. In Jesus' Name, Amen.

AFFIRMATION:

I am compassionate and understanding.

DAY 159: *Understanding*

"But if I do His work, believe in the evidence of the miraculous works I have done, even if you don't believe me. Then you will know and understand that the Father is in me, and I am in the Father."
John 10:38

PRAYER:
Dear Lord, I pray for patience and understanding that I may walk in Your ways rather than my own ways, and Your thoughts than my thoughts. Lord, let my lifestyle be a reflection of You. Let patience have its way within my heart. I thank You in advance for patience and understanding. Amen.

AFFIRMATION:
I am teachable and understanding.

DAY 160: *Understanding*

"So we have not stopped praying for you since we first heard about you. We ask God to give you complete knowledge of His will and to give you spiritual wisdom and understanding. Then the way you live will always honor and please the Lord, and your lives will produce every kind of good fruit. All the while, you will grow as you learn to know God better and better."

Colossians 1:9-10

PRAYER:

Dear Lord Jesus, grant me the gift of understanding. Help me to understand the things I need to know. Help me, Lord, to always see You at work. Thank you for sending the Holy Spirit to live in me and to lead and guide me into all truth. Amen.

AFFIRMATION:

I seek to know God and to having an understanding of His will for my life.

DAY 161: *Understanding*

"For ever since the world was created, people have seen the earth and sky. Through everything God made, they can clearly see His invisible qualities - His eternal power and divine nature. So they have no excuse for not knowing God."

Romans 1:20

PRAYER:

Dear Father God, I pray, Lord, that You would give me a deeper understanding of Your Word. I pray that you will open the eyes of my heart as I study and meditate on Your word. Give me the understanding to see Your way. Bless me with patience to wait upon You, Lord. Amen.

AFFIRMATION:

I have great understanding and the ability to study and learn.

WEEK 24: *Love*

DAY 162: *Love*

"For God so loved the world, that He gave His only begotten Son,
that whosoever believeth in Him should not perish, but have everlasting life."
John 3:16

PRAYER:

Father God, I thank You for loving me. I thank You for Your Darling Son Jesus. You have been taking care of my family and me. I may not know what You are doing. I trust You while I wait. Grant me the will to go on, the will to live again. In Jesus' Name, Amen.

AFFIRMATION:

Love is all around me. I receive love from others.

DAY 163: *Love*

"There is no greater love than to lay down one's life for one's friends."
John 15:13

PRAYER:
Dear Father God, we thank You for Your Darling Son, Jesus. We thank You for the gift of life. You have shown us what love looks like. May we be a reflection of Your love. Help us to love well, dear Father. In Jesus' Name, Amen.

AFFIRMATION:
My heart is full of love.

DAY 164: *Love*

"Three things will last forever: faith, hope, and love, and the greatest of these is love."
1 Corinthians 13:13

PRAYER:

Dear Jesus, we thank You for many blessings. Lord, we ask You to bless and fill our family with love. We pray for Your kindness and mercy. The Lord is compassionate and gracious, slow to anger, abounding in love. Help us to extend love and kindness to others. In Jesus' Name, Amen.

AFFIRMATION:

I am loveable.

DAY 165: *Love*

"Love is patient and kind. Love is not jealous or boastful or proud or rude. It does not demand its own way, it's not irritable, and keeps no record of being wronged. It does not rejoice about injustice but rejoices whenever the truth wins out. Love never gives up,
never loses faith, is always hopeful, and endures through every circumstance."
1 Corinthians 13:4-7

PRAYER:
Dear Lord, I come into Your presence with thanksgiving. You are my teacher. I thank You that there is no human experience that I might walk through where Your love cannot reach me. I am thankful for Your love. In Jesus' Name, Amen.

AFFIRMATION:
Love is my priority.

___

___

___

___

___

___

___

___

___

___

___

___

___

___

___

DAY 166: *Love*

"And do everything with love."

1 Corinthians 16:14

PRAYER:

Dear God, our Father, help us to love ourselves so much that we forgive anyone who has ever hurt us in our life. Give us the courage to love our family and friends unconditionally. Today is a new beginning. Help us to begin our day with love. My day begins with thoughts of You and ends with prayer. Teach us, dear Lord, to do everything with love. In Jesus' Name, Amen.

AFFIRMATION:

I emanate love.

DAY 167: *Love*

"Most important of all, continue to show deep love
for each other, for love covers a multitude of sins."
1 Peter 4:8

PRAYER:

Dear Lord, please work on me that I may love other people with all my heart. I pray that everyone will experience your genuine love. Help me to love without condition and expectation, to love others simply because You love me, and not because of what others do. Fill my heart with the love that You freely give. Help me love as abundantly as You have loved me. Amen.

AFFIRMATION:

I give love to others and others give it to me.

DAY 168: *Love*

"But anyone who does not love does not know God, for God is love."
1 John 4:8

PRAYER:

Dear Lord, bless us with love; that we may love as You love! Teach us to walk in Your attributes with love and kindness. Help us to treat others as we would like to be treated. You are the ultimate example of love, and we are so grateful for that. In Jesus' Holy Name, we pray, Amen.

AFFIRMATION:

I spread love, and it returns to me.

WEEK 25: *Patience*

DAY 169: *Patience*

"But the Holy Spirit produces this kind of fruit in our lives:
love, joy, peace, patience, kindness, goodness, faithfulness,
gentleness, and self-control. There is no law against these things!"
Galatians 5:22, 23

PRAYER:

Dear Lord, please help me to be patient with great understanding. I pray that here on earth I reflect You in all ways and that Your understanding will govern my behavior. I will seek You for my wisdom and my understanding. Thank You, Lord. Amen.

AFFIRMATION:

I treat myself with love, patience, and compassion.

DAY 170: *Patience*

"Love is patient and kind. Love is not jealous or boastful or proud or rude. It does not demand its own way. It is not irritable, and it keeps no record of being wronged."

1 Corinthians 13:4-5

PRAYER:

Dear Lord, I call upon You and know that You will answer me. I thank You for divine understanding that reveals to me the things I do not understand. I pray for patience and understanding in all areas of my life. I thank You for allowing me to see things like You do. Amen.

AFFIRMATION:

Practicing patience is my priority.

DAY 171: *Patience*

"Rejoice in our confident hope. Be patient in trouble, and keep on praying. When God's people are in need, be ready to help them. Always be eager to practice hospitality. Bless those who persecute you. Don't cure them. Be happy with those who are happy, and weep with those who weep."

Romans 12:12-15

PRAYER:

Dear Lord, thank You for instructing me and teaching me in the way I should go. I pray that my patience and understanding comes from You. Thank You, Lord. Amen.

AFFIRMATION:

I am full of patience and peace.

DAY 172: *Patience*

"I waited patiently for the Lord to help me, and He turned to me and heard my cry."
Psalm 40:1

PRAYER:

Dear Lord, I wait patiently for You because I know that You who began a good work in me, is faithful to complete it within me. Increase my understanding when life becomes difficult. I pray that even in my affliction, I wait patiently. I declare that I will remain joyful in hope and faithful in prayer. Amen.

AFFIRMATION:

I am thankful for my ability to wait patiently.

DAY 173: *Patience*

"But if we look forward to something we don't yet have, we must wait patiently and confidently."
Romans 8:25

PRAYER:

Dear Lord, I pray for an outpouring of patience, divine understanding, and revelation in my life. I pray that I learn to wait patiently with understanding for all things to come to pass in my life. Amen.

AFFIRMATION:

I choose to wait patiently.

DAY 174: *Patience*

"Since God chose You to be a holy people He loves, you must clothe yourselves with tenderhearted mercy, kindness, humility, gentleness, and patience."
Colossians 3:12

PRAYER:
Dear Lord, teach me to be patient with life and with people. Give me the ability to learn from You and model Your patience with others around me. Help me to be more like You in the ways that I talk, act, and live. Thank You, Lord. Amen.

AFFIRMATION:
Everyday I learn to be more patient.

DAY 175: *Patience*

"Dear brothers and sisters, be patient as you wait for the Lord's return.
Consider the farmers who patiently wait for the rains in the fall and in the spring.
They eagerly look for the valuable harvest to ripen. You, too, must be patient.
Take courage, for the coming of the Lord is near."
James 5:7-8

PRAYER:
Dear Lord, I trust You. No one knows when You will return. It's my duty and responsibility to be ready when You come. In the meanwhile, I will wait patiently for Your return. I have a message to deliver to Your people. You must be born again. I will work at living in peace with everyone, and work at living a holy life, for those who are not holy will not see the Lord. Amen.

AFFIRMATION:
I embrace patience as a virtue that brings me peace.

WEEK 26: *Faith*

DAY 176: *Faith*

"In addition to all of these, hold up the shield of faith to stop the fiery arrows of the devil. Put on salvation as your helmet, and take the sword of the spirit, which is the Word of God."

Ephesians 6:16-17

PRAYER:

Lord, please increase my faith in You. Help me to trust in Your love and Your plan for my life. Give me the strength to have confidence in Your goodness and Your grace. I pray for Your guidance and direction in my life. Bless me, dear Lord, with Your peace. In Jesus' Name, Amen.

AFFIRMATION:

I walk by faith and not by sight.

DAY 177: *Faith*

"God saved you by grace when you believed. And you can't take credit for this; it is a gift from God. Salvation is not a reward for the good things we have done, so none of us boast about it."
Ephesians 2:8-9

PRAYER:
Precious Lord, I thank You every day for the faith You instilled in me. It is through this faith that I continue to receive Your grace. You have blessed me over and over again. But the greatest gift I have ever received was the faith I have devoted to You. Thank You, Lord, for the gift of faith. Amen.

AFFIRMATION:
I surrender to God and trust His wisdom.

DAY 178: *Faith*

"My old self has been crucified with Christ. It is no longer I who live, but Christ lives in me. So I live in this earthly body by trusting in the Son of God who loved me and gave Himself for me."

Galatians 2:20

PRAYER:

Dear Lord, right now, I yield to the truth that I am weak, and you are strong. You are my strength today. When I am weary, tired, or heavily burdened, I can depend on You. Your hiding place is secure. Thank You, Lord, for being my refuge. Amen.

AFFIRMATION:

In my faith, I find salvation.

DAY 179: *Faith*

"And Jesus said to him, 'Go, for your faith has healed you.'
Instantly, the man could see, and he followed Jesus down the road."
Mark 10:52

PRAYER:

Dear Lord, I put my trust and my faith in You, because I know that nothing is impossible with You. I believe that You are my healer. Lord, let my faith never stray from You, for I already have everything I could ever want by being a follower of Christ. Amen.

AFFIRMATION:

Faith is the foundation of my life.

DAY 180: *Faith*

"'You don't have enough faith,' Jesus told them. 'I tell you the truth, if you have faith even as small as a mustard seed, you could say to this mountain, move from here to there, and it would move. Nothing would be impossible.'"

Matthew 17:20

PRAYER:

Dear Lord, I receive the grace to endure all the challenges and hardships I am going through. Your Word says faith comes from hearing and hearing the Word of God. Lord, give me the heart that longs for Your Word and spirit. Let my faith grow from a small faith to a greater faith. In Jesus' Name, Amen.

AFFIRMATION:

My faith crushes my fears.

DAY 181: *Faith*

"Therefore, since we have been made right in God's sight by faith, we have peace with God because of what Jesus Christ our Lord has done for us. Because of our faith, Christ has brought us into this place of undeserved privilege where we now stand, and we confidently and joyfully look forward to sharing God's glory."

Romans 5:1-2

PRAYER:

Dear Father God, I come before You with a prayer of faith. I lift up my voice to You, seeking Your guidance, protection, and mercy. Guide me according to Your perfect will, and help me to align my desires with Your purpose. May my life be a reflection of Your grace. In Jesus' Name, I pray. Amen.

AFFIRMATION:

I choose faith over fear and peace over perfection.

DAY 182: *Faith*

"This Good News tells us how God makes us right in His sight.
This is accomplished from start to finish by faith. As the scripture says,
'It is through faith that a righteous person has life'."
Romans 1:17

PRAYER:

Dear Lord, You are my Strong Tower, Deliverer, and Shelter. You say that the righteous man will live by faith. Fill my heart with faith in You. Keep my eyes fixed on You and You alone. Lord, increase my faith in You. For You are my God. Amen.

AFFIRMATION:

"Faith is awakened in me now."

WEEK 27: *Carrying Your Cross*

DAY 183: *Carrying Your Cross*

"Then Pilate turned Jesus over to be crucified. So they took Jesus away. Carrying the cross by himself, he went to the Place of the Skull (in Hebrew, Golgotha)."

John 19:16-17

PRAYER:

Dear Lord, Jesus, I know that following You will not always be easy. I embrace with love as I carry my cross. Please give me the strength and faith to persevere so that I may bring glory to Your Name. Amen.

AFFIRMATION:

If I am to share God's glory, I also must share in His suffering.

DAY 184: *Carrying Your Cross*

"We do this by keeping our eyes on Jesus, the Champion who initiates and perfects our faith. Because of the joy awaiting Him, He endured the cross, disregarding its shame. Now He is seated in the place of honor beside God's throne."
Hebrews 12:2

PRAYER:
Dear Lord, You are our champion. You endured the cross for mankind. We thank You, Lord, for enduring the cross and completing Your mission here on earth. We pray for grace to carry a heavy cross. It's a privilege and honor to serve the Lord. Amen.

AFFIRMATION:
It's an honor to follow Jesus.

DAY 185: *Carrying Your Cross*

"And if you do not carry Your own cross and follow me, you cannot be my disciple."
Luke 14:27

PRAYER:
Heavenly Father, we pray that we will carry our cross and follow Your Son, Jesus. Lord, You promised that You would be there to help us bear it. Lord, You are faithful. We thank You for the grace to carry our cross. In Jesus' name, Amen.

AFFIRMATION:
I take pleasure in my weaknesses, and in the results, hardships, persecutions, and troubles that I suffer for Christ.

DAY 186: *Carrying Your Cross*

"When they were finally tired of mocking Him, they took off the robe and put His own clothes on Him again. Then they led Him away to be crucified. Along the way, they came across a man named Simon, who was from Cyrene, and the soldiers forced Him to carry Jesus' cross."

Matthew 27:31-32

PRAYER:

Dear Lord, as Christians, we are to follow Jesus each and every day. There are times when that is not so easy. Father, we thank You for Your Son, Jesus. Lord, help us to follow in His footsteps and take up our crosses daily. Help us to deny ourselves every day. In Jesus' Name, Amen.

AFFIRMATION:

Yet, what we suffer now is nothing compared to the glory He will reveal to us later.

DAY 187: *Carrying Your Cross*

"If You refuse to take up Your cross and follow me, You are not worthy of being mine."
Matthew 10:38

PRAYER:

Our Father, who art in heaven, hallowed be Thy Name. Thy Kingdom come. Thy will be done, on earth as it is in Heaven. We are thankful for Your Son, Jesus. Our prayer is that You will give us the strength to carry our cross. Jesus endured the cross. Jesus was obedient to the Father. Help us, dear Lord, to be obedient as well. In Jesus' Name, Amen.

AFFIRMATION:

I decided to pick up my cross and to follow Jesus.

DAY 188: *Carrying Your Cross*

"Then He said to the crowd, 'If any of you wants to be my follower, you must give up your way, take up your cross daily, and follow me.'"

Luke 9:23

PRAYER:

Dear Lord, the storms keep on raging in my life. It feels like I'm carrying the weight of the world on my shoulders. I know that You are with me. My pain has purpose. I have decided to deny myself and trust God's will in all things. It may be difficult, but I must carry my cross. In Jesus' Name, Amen.

AFFIRMATION:

People will know me for my strength.

DAY 189: *Carrying Your Cross*

"See my servant prosper; he will be highly exalted. But many were amazed when they saw him. His face was so disfigured. He seemed hardly human, and from his appearance, one would scarcely know he was a man."
Isaiah 52:13-14

PRAYER:

Dear Jesus, thank You for fulfilling Your mission here on earth. You were unrecognizable after everything You endured. Yet, Your mission was accomplished. Lord, You carried Your cross of pain and suffering. It was a heavy cross. Thank You, Lord, for everything You have done. Amen.

AFFIRMATION:

My decision has been made. I must follow Jesus.

WEEK 28: *Healing*

DAY 190: *Healing*

"'I will give you back your health and heal your wounds,' says the Lord.
'For you are called an outcast Jerusalem for whom no one cares.'"
Jeremiah 30:17

PRAYER:

Our Father, You are my healer. My body is healed. I thank You for my healing. My faith is in You. There is nothing too hard for my God. In Jesus' Name, I pray. Amen.

AFFIRMATION:

My body is the temple of God.

DAY 191: *Healing*

"He sent out His word and healed them, snatching them from the door of death. Let them praise the Lord for His great love and for the wonderful things He has done for them."

Psalm 107:20-21

PRAYER:

Dear Lord, thank You for Your healing power. I thank You for my healing now. I receive and believe by faith my miracle of being healed and made whole. In Jesus' Name, Amen.

AFFIRMATION:

My healing is now.

DAY 192: *Healing*

"The Lord is close to the brokenhearted; He rescues those whose spirits are crushed."

Psalm 34:18

PRAYER:

Dear Lord, help me to release my shame and grief freely to You. I am heartbroken and feel so alone. I need You to comfort me. Jesus, I ask that You take this pain and use it for Your good, that through the struggle of my heartbreak, I would find myself closer to You than ever before. In Jesus' Name, Amen.

AFFIRMATION:

I let go of my perceived pain.

DAY 193: *Healing*

"My health may fail, and my spirit may grow weak,
but God remains the strength of my heart; He is mine forever."
Psalm 73:26

PRAYER:

Heavenly Father, I come before You today in need of Your healing hand. In You, all things are possible. Guide me towards better health, and give me the wisdom to identify those You've placed around me to help me get better. In Jesus' Name, I pray. Amen.

AFFIRMATION:

I am healthy, happy, and radiant.

DAY 194: *Healing*

"This is my comfort in my affliction: for Thy word hath quickened me."
Psalm 119:50

PRAYER:

Oh God, Your love has held me and kept me through this suffering. Heal me, oh Lord, and I'll be healed. Be near me in my time of weakness and pain; sustain me by Your grace that my strength and courage may not fail; heal me according to Your will. I pray all of these things, in Your Name. Amen.

AFFIRMATION:

I give myself permission to heal.

DAY 195: *Healing*

"Yet, it was our weaknesses He carried; it was our sorrows that weighed Him down. And we thought His troubles were a punishment for His own sins! But He was pierced for our rebellion, crushed for our sins. He was beaten so we could be whole. He was whipped so we could be healed."

Isaiah 53:4-5

PRAYER:

Dear Lord, I believe that there is no illness You cannot heal. You have provided for our healing through the death of Jesus Christ. For Your Word declares, by His stripes we were healed. In Jesus' Name, Amen.

AFFIRMATION:

I am thriving in my healing journey.

DAY 196: *Healing*

"Have compassion on me, Lord, for I am weak.
Heal me, Lord, for my bones are in agony."
Psalm 6:2

PRAYER:

Dear Lord, touch me now with Your healing hands. Have mercy on me, Lord, for I am faint. You are Jehovah-Rapha, the God who heals. I receive my healing. Give me the faith to walk in freedom and victory. In Jesus' Name, Amen.

AFFIRMATION:

I am worthy of good health.

WEEK 29: *Strength*

DAY 197: *Strength*

"For I can do everything through Christ who gives me strength."

Philippians 4:13

PRAYER:

Dear Lord, I have been trying to weather the storms of life. I need Your power and strength to face each one. Give me the strength and power that I know can only come from You. I thank You for it. Amen.

AFFIRMATION:

I choose to be strong.

DAY 198: *Strength*

"The Lord is my strength and my song; He has given me victory.
This is my God, and I will praise Him - my Father's God, I will exalt Him!"
Exodus 15:2

PRAYER:
Dear Lord, I ask You to give me strength to help others. Help me to help others. Give me strength to live according to the Golden Rule, enthusiasm to inspire those around me. Amen.

AFFIRMATION:
All of my strength comes from the Lord.

DAY 199: *Strength*

"See, God has come to save me. I will trust in Him and not be afraid.
The Lord God is my strength and my song; He has given me victory."
Isaiah 12:2

PRAYER:

Oh God, please give me strength when I am weak. For when I am at my weakest, Your strength is strongest. Teach me, oh God, to rely on Your strength, not my own. Thank You for working in my weakness and pouring Your strength into me. Amen.

AFFIRMATION:

I choose to be strong.

DAY 200: *Strength*

"My health may fail, and my spirit may grow weak,
but God remains the strength of my heart; He is mine forever."
Psalm 73:26

PRAYER:

Dear Lord, I thank You for being my strength and my shield. I know You are the source of my strength and my Great Comforter. Thank You for never leaving or forsaking me. Your abiding presence is my source of hope. Amen.

AFFIRMATION:

My strength is not just physical, but also mental and emotional.

DAY 201: *Strength*

"Each time He said, 'My grace is all you need. My power works best in weakness.' So now I am glad to boast about my weakness, so that the power of Christ can work through me."

2 Corinthians 12:9

PRAYER:

Dear Lord, You are my strength like no other. I thank You for the strength You have given me. The Lord is our refuge and strength, an ever present help in trouble. Thank You Lord for giving me strength. Amen.

AFFIRMATION:

My strength allows me to stand and to watch God.

DAY 202: *Strength*

"Then he said unto them, 'Go your way, eat the fat, and drink the sweet, and send portions unto them for whom nothing is prepared: for this day is holy unto our Lord: neither be ye sorry; for the joy of the Lord is your strength'."

Nehemiah 8:10

PRAYER:

Dear Lord, You are my strength. Even in my weakness, You have made me strong. I will forever look to You. Help me to rise above any difficult situation. Let Your words of strength be on my mind and lips each day. Grant me the strength that I need. Amen.

AFFIRMATION:

Choosing to remain positive is my most powerful form of strength.

DAY 203: *Strength*

"Rejoice in our confident hope. Be patient in trouble, and keep on praying."

Romans 12:12

PRAYER:

Dear Lord, Your Word says that when we wait on You, Lord, You will renew our strength. I trust in Your infinite capacity of strength. Thank You for pouring Your strength into me. Amen.

AFFIRMATION:

I am strong and resilient.

WEEK 30: *Suffering*

DAY 204: *Suffering*

"God blesses those who are persecuted for doing right, for the Kingdom of Heaven is theirs. God blesses you when people mock you and persecute you and lie about you and say all sorts of evil things against you because you are my followers. Be happy about it! Be very glad! For a great reward awaits you in heaven. And remember, the ancient prophets were persecuted in the same way."

Matthew 5:10-12

PRAYER:

Dear Lord, thank You for Your loving kindness and compassion. Thank You that You will never forsake us nor leave us comfortless. We have gone through much suffering. We hold firm to Your promises. We praise You, Lord, that You are our Strong Tower, into whose everlasting arm we flee for protection and safety. Lord, You are our Protector. We thank You, in Jesus, Amen.

AFFIRMATION:

We are willing to be at peace with everyone and ourself.

DAY 205: *Suffering*

"Your promise revives me; it comforts me in all my troubles."

Psalm 119:50

PRAYER:

Dear Lord, I am thankful for every promise. I believe every promise is true. I'm troubled on every side, yet not distressed; we are perplexed, but not in despair. Persecuted but not destroyed. Your promises revive me, it comforts me in all my troubles. Be my Comforter, my Healer, and bring me peace. In Jesus' Name, Amen.

AFFIRMATION:

I am forgiven and free from sin and guilt.

DAY 206: *Suffering*

"And since we are His children, we are His heirs. In fact, together with Christ we are heirs of God's glory. But if we are to share His glory, we must also share His sufferings. Yet, what we suffer now is nothing compared to the glory He will reveal to us later."

Romans 8:17-18

PRAYER:

Dear Lord, in everything, I give You praise. The suffering of this present time is not worthy to be compared to the glory which shall be revealed in us. I believe the Lord. I give Him praise in Jesus' Name, Amen.

AFFIRMATION:

I am chosen and called by God.

DAY 207: *Suffering*

"He was despised and rejected, a man of sorrows, acquainted with deepest grief. We turned our backs on Him and looked the other way. He was despised, and we did not care."

Isaiah 53:3

PRAYER:

Dear Lord of Heaven's Armies, You sent Your Son to show us that there is a reward for those who last to the end. Oh Lord, lead them beside quiet waters and refresh their soul. Guide them along the right paths and comfort them in this dark time. Shine Your face on their suffering. Bless them and turn their tears into laughter. In Jesus' Holy Name, Amen.

AFFIRMATION:

I am a Partaker of the Suffering of Christ.

DAY 208: *Suffering*

"We can rejoice, too, when we run into problems and trials,
for we know that they help us develop endurance. And endurance develops
strength of character, and character strengthens our confident hope of salvation.
And this hope will not lead to disappointment. For we know how dearly God loves us,
because He has given us the Holy Spirit to fill our hearts with His love."
Romans 5:3-5

PRAYER:

Dear Lord, I love You with every fiber of my heart. I'm going through a difficult time. I've cried out to You, and my hope is in the Lord. I will keep my eyes on You today and forever, in Jesus' Name.

AFFIRMATION:

My hardships bring me opportunities to promote God.

DAY 209: *Suffering*

"In His kindness, God called you to share in His eternal glory by means of Christ Jesus. So after you have suffered a little while, He will restore, support, and strengthen you, and He will place you on a firm foundation."

1 Peter 5:10

PRAYER:

Dear Lord, I thank You for all the blessings that are prepared for me. I receive restoration, support, and new strength today in Jesus' Holy Name, I pray. Amen.

AFFIRMATION:

I trust that everything in my life is unfolding perfectly.

DAY 210: *Suffering*

"For the more we suffer for Christ, the more God will shower us with His comfort through Christ."

2 Corinthians 1:5

PRAYER:

Dear Lord, You are our Comforter. So many of Your children are going through suffering physically, mentally, and emotionally. You are our blessed hope. Let Your unfailing love be with us, Lord, even as we put our hope in You. In Jesus' Name, Amen.

AFFIRMATION:

We are justified and redeemed by God.

WEEK 31: *Endurance*

DAY 211: *Endurance*

"This is a trustworthy saying: If we die in Him, we will also live with Him.
If we endure hardship, we will reign with Him. If we deny Him, He will deny us.
If we are unfaithful, He remains faithful, for He cannot deny who He is."
2 Timothy 2:11-13

PRAYER:

Dear Lord, through Your love, we can endure and overcome all things. Help me to be diligent and carry on. Strengthen my heart in times of persecution and suffering. Give me the grace to serve You faithfully and fully. In Jesus' Name, Amen.

AFFIRMATION:

I am a winner.

DAY 212: *Endurance*

"So let it grow, for when your endurance is fully developed, you will be perfect and complete, needing nothing."
James 1:4

PRAYER:
Dear Lord, help me to never become tired of doing good things. As I grow closer to You, give me the endurance to serve and love others. Endurance is a gift from God mentioned. I thank you for empowering me to endure. Amen.

AFFIRMATION:
Christ endured and so will I.

DAY 213: *Endurance*

"So let's not get tired of doing what is good. At just the right time, we will reap a harvest of blessing if we don't give up."
Galatians 6:9

PRAYER:

Dear Lord, I ask that I would be strengthened with all power according to Your glorious might so that I may have great endurance and patience. We can endure all things because Jesus has overcome all things. Amen.

AFFIRMATION:

I am fortified and strong.

DAY 214: *Endurance*

"This means that God's holy people must endure persecution patiently, obeying His commands and maintaining their faith in Jesus."
Revelation 14:12

PRAYER:
Dear Lord, please continue to help guide and protect me throughout this trying situation. Grant me Your strength so I might endure the tests that are waiting for me. For every challenge, I see Your mercy. Lord Jesus, I am thankful for the gift of endurance. In Jesus' Name, Amen.

AFFIRMATION:
I have an enduring spirit.

DAY 215: *Endurance*

"Therefore, since we are surrounded by such a huge crowd of witnesses to the life of faith, let us strip off every weight that slows us down, especially the sin that so easily trips us up. And let us run with endurance the race God has set before us."

Hebrews 12:1

PRAYER:

Dear Lord, I count it a blessing when I go through trials and temptations, because I know my faith is being tested to produce perseverance. Thank You for the endurance You provide, empowering us to withstand life's trials. Lord, You are my sustainer. I find strength to endure, the courage to persevere, and the hope to thrive. Amen.

AFFIRMATION:

My eyes are fixed on Jesus, and I am enduring well.

DAY 216: *Endurance*

"For God is pleased when, conscious of His will, you patiently endure unjust treatment. Of course, you get no credit for being patient if you are beaten for doing wrong. But if you suffer for doing good and endure it patiently, God is pleased with you."

1 Peter 2:19-20

PRAYER:

Dear Jesus, my Lord, I pray to You today in supplication for endurance and patience. Carry me through this trial as I endure as a soldier. May Your wisdom shine through me as I proclaim Your Word. Help me to endure through all struggles and trials in Jesus' Name. Amen.

AFFIRMATION:

The spirit of the Lord has empowered me to endure.

DAY 217: *Endurance*

"As you endure this divine discipline, remember that God is treating you as His own children. Whoever heard of a child who is never disciplined by its father?"

Hebrews 12:7

PRAYER:

Our Father, in times of trouble and sorrow, I look to You Lord for guidance. You've kept me safe in times of danger. You are my shelter. With You I can endure any storm. I will praise You while I'm enduring the storm. In Jesus' Name, I pray. Amen.

AFFIRMATION:

God has anointed me to endure.

WEEK 32: *Enduring*

DAY 218: *Enduring*

"When Job prayed for his friends, the Lord restored his fortunes. In fact, the Lord gave him twice as much as before. Then all his brothers, sisters, and former friends came and feasted with him in his home. And they consoled him and comforted him because of all the trials the Lord had brought against him. And each of them brought him a gift of money and a gold ring."

Job 42: 10-11

PRAYER:

Dear God, You are amazing. I thank You for giving me the strength to endure while the storm was raging. Thank You for providing all of my needs. In Jesus' Name, Amen.

AFFIRMATION:

I practice gratitude for all that I have and all that is coming.

DAY 219: *Enduring*

"If you follow this advice, and if God commands you to do so, then you will be able to endure the pressures, and all these people will go home in peace."

Exodus 18:23

PRAYER:

Our Lord, I stand before You humbled by Your majesty and Your unwavering love. Please grant me the endurance to face life's trials and tribulations. Help me to embrace my struggles as an opportunity to grow in Your grace. In Jesus' Name, Amen.

AFFIRMATION:

I am brave as I am enduring.

DAY 220: *Enduring*

"So let's not get tired of doing what is good. At just the right time we will reap a harvest of blessing if we don't give up."
Galatians 6:9

PRAYER:
Heavenly Father, You are my strength. Your hand upholds me, Your grace sustains me, Your power keeps me. Thank You, Lord, for Your enduring power. In Jesus' Name, I pray. Amen.

AFFIRMATIONS:
I'm enduring, and I will achieve all of my goals.

DAY 221: *Enduring*

"We can rejoice, too, when we run into problems and trials, for we know that they help us develop endurance. And endurance develops strength of character, and character strengthens our confident hope of salvation."

Romans 5:3-4

PRAYER:

Merciful Father, I thank You for the trials and tribulations that I have gone through. Surely, I have endured much. Endurance has developed me to be strong and courageous. It has built my character. I am confident that You are my Great Hope. In Jesus' Name, I pray. Amen.

AFFIRMATION:

I am fearlessly enduring.

DAY 222: *Enduring*

"We also pray that you will be strengthened with all His glorious power so you will have all the endurance and patience you need. May you be filled with joy."

Colossians 1:11

PRAYER:

Oh God, I am in a difficult phase in my life. I know that You are with me. I ask You today to renew my strength. I am weak. I don't want to give up. I am counting on You to bring me through. In Jesus' Name, I pray. Amen.

AFFIRMATION:

I am strong, and I will endure with the strength that You have given me.

DAY 223: *Enduring*

"Patient endurance is what you need now, so that you will continue to do God's will. Then you will receive all that He has promised."
Hebrews 10:36

PRAYER:
Dear Lord, I give You praise in the midst of the storm. I will give you adorations. This storm will cease. You have given me enduring power. I am more than a conqueror through Christ Jesus. Amen.

AFFIRMATION:
I am enduring with patience.

DAY 224: *Enduring*

"For you know that when your faith is tested, your endurance has a chance to grow. So let it grow, for when your endurance is fully developed, you will be perfect and complete, needing nothing."
James 1:3-4

PRAYER:
Dear Jesus, Lord I thank You for giving me strength when I am weak, love when I feel forsaken, courage when I am afraid, hope when I am in distress. Lord, I am forever thankful in Jesus' Name, I pray. Amen.

AFFIRMATION:
I have everything I need to succeed.

WEEK 33: *Wounds*

DAY 225: *Wounds*

"They stripped Him and put a scarlet robe on Him. They wove thorn branches into a crown and put it on His head, and they placed a reed stick in His right hand as a scepter. Then they knelt before Him in mockery and taunted, 'Hail! King of the Jews'."

Matthew 27:28-29

PRAYER:

Dear Lord, You paid the price for my salvation. I am thankful that You made a way for me. You went through terrible suffering. I invite You into this broken place within me, these open wounds. I give You total access to my heart. Walk closely beside me during my journey to healing and recovery that I know is possible through Your power alone. In Jesus' name, Amen.

AFFIRMATION:

I am strong, resilient, and capable of overcoming any obstacle.

DAY 226: *Wounds*

"He heals the brokenhearted and bandages their wounds."

Psalm 147:3

PRAYER:

Dear Lord, please wrap me up in Your healing. I want to see Your handiwork. Here are my wounds, Lord. Please show me Your power. Thank You for healing me and putting all the pieces of my heart back together again. I trust You, Lord, and I rely on You for complete healing. In Jesus' Name, Amen.

AFFIRMATION:

I receive my healing today.

DAY 227: *Wounds*

"My enemies surround me like a pack of dogs; an evil gang closes in on me. They have pierced my hands and feet."
Psalm 22:16

PRAYER:
Heavenly Father, I call on You right now in a special way. Jesus prayed for His enemies on the cross. I am so grateful that Jesus showed us how to pray for our enemies. Today, I pray for all of my enemies. Father, forgive them, for they do not know what they are doing. In the name of Jesus, I pray. Amen.

AFFIRMATION:
I forgive them all this day.

DAY 228: *Wounds*

"But He was wounded for our transgressions, He was bruised for our iniquities: the chastisement of our peace was upon Him; with His stripes we are healed."

Isaiah 53:5

PRAYER:

Dear Lord, I thank You for the manifestation of Your healing power. Today my faith is in You. I believe that You were wounded for our transgressions. So today I receive my healing, my faith in Jesus' Name. Amen.

AFFIRMATION:

By His stripes, I am healed, in Jesus' Name.

DAY 229: *Wounds*

"My back is covered with cuts, as if a farmer had plowed long furrows."
Psalm 129:3

PRAYER:
Heavenly Father, in the name of Jesus, I come before You just as I am; I repent of my sins. Please forgive me. I forgive all others for what they have done against me. Give me back the health and strength I need. I feel weak and find it hard to carry on. I pray this in Jesus' Name, Amen.

AFFIRMATION:
I declare that my healing is already in process.

DAY 230: *Wounds*

"And if someone asks, 'Then what about those wounds on your chest?' He will say, 'I was wounded at my friends house!'"

Zechariah 13:6

PRAYER:

Dear Lord, Heal me, oh Lord, and I shall be healed; save me, and I shall be saved. For You are my praise. I pray that Your plans and purpose will be carried out for Your greater praise and glory. I ask this in Jesus' Name, Amen.

AFFIRMATION:

I am worthy to be cared for.

DAY 231: *Wounds*

"But one of the soldiers with a spear pierced
His side, and forthwith came there out blood and water."
John 19:34

PRAYER:

Dear Lord, one of the soldiers with a spear pierced Your side and blood and water came out. This was the final wound. I am so grateful for all You endured for mankind. You fulfilled purpose and destiny. I want to fulfill all that You have called me to do; I want to leave no stone unturned in my lifetime. Order my steps dear Lord, according to Your will, Amen.

AFFIRMATION:

I accept myself, I love myself, and I'm healed.

WEEK 34: *Victory*

DAY 232: *Victory*

"I have told you all this so that you may have peace in me. Here on earth you will have many trials and sorrows. But take heart, because I have overcome the world."

John 16:33

PRAYER:

Dear Jesus, You are my victory. I claim You today over every area of my life. Your victory is assured. Lord, You never fail. I am victorious through Christ Jesus, Amen.

AFFIRMATION:

I will let my light shine everywhere I go.

DAY 233: *Victory*

"But thank God! He gives us victory over sin and death through our Lord Jesus Christ."

1 Corinthians 15:57

PRAYER:

Dear Lord, thank You for the victory that is mine through the resurrection of Your Son. I want to be more like Jesus. I am an overcomer through Christ Jesus. Amen.

AFFIRMATION:

I know that I can achieve anything I want to.

DAY 234: *Victory*

"What shall we say about such wonderful things as these?
If God is for us, who can ever be against us?"
Romans 8:31

PRAYER:

Dear God, I know that You will fight every battle for me. I need Your victory in my situation. For the battle belongs to You, Lord, and You alone promise victory. In the victorious name of Jesus, I pray. Amen.

AFFIRMATIONS:

Destined for victory.

DAY 235: *Victory*

"For the Lord your God is going with you! He will fight for you against your enemies, and He will give victory!"
Deuteronomy 20:14

PRAYER:

Heavenly Father, we give You thanks through our Lord Jesus Christ. You have given us a spiritual victory over all the plots of the enemy. We pray that You would rule and reign in our life, so that we may live to Your praise and glory. In Jesus' Name, Amen.

AFFIRMATION:

There are no limits to what we can achieve.

DAY 236: *Victory*

"For God so loved the world, that He gave His only begotten Son,
that whosoever believeth in Him, shall not perish, but have everlasting life."
John 3:16

PRAYER:
Dear God, please strengthen me for this journey. Thank You for the victory that is mine through the resurrection of Your Son Jesus.

AFFIRMATION:
Confidence and strength pave victorious journeys.

DAY 237: *Victory*

"Be strong in the Lord and in His mighty power. Put on all God's armor so that You will be able to stand firm against all strategies of the devil."

Ephesians 6:10-11

PRAYER:

Dear Lord, I have some enemies. I cry out to You for deliverance from my enemies. I need Your help! I thank You for Your infinite mercy, and I ask for Your absolute protection against evil and all of them who want to hurt me. In Jesus' Name, Amen.

AFFIRMATION:

I admire my capabilities.

DAY 238: *Victory*

"No, despite all these things, overwhelming victory is ours through Christ who loved us."

Romans 8:37

PRAYER:

Dear Lord, thank You for victory. Through it all, You have shown Yourself to be mighty. For I know that You are working everything together for my good. Help me trust You even at this time. I believe that these things too must pass. In Jesus' Name, Amen.

AFFIRMATION:

I am capable of achieving greatness.

WEEK 35: *Promise*

DAY 239: *Promise*

"No one will be able to stand against you as long as you live.
For I will be with you as I was with Moses. I will not fail you or abandon you."
Joshua 1:5

PRAYER:

Our Father who art in heaven, hallowed be Thy name; Thy Kingdom come, Thy will be done, on earth as it is in Heaven. I am forever grateful for the multitude of blessings that You have bestowed upon me. You are with me always. I am strong and no one will be able to stand against me. Thank You, Lord, in Jesus' Name, I pray. Amen.

AFFIRMATION:

For the Lord is with me, and He fights all of my battles.

DAY 240: *Promise*

"Then Jesus said, 'Come to me,
all of you who are weary and carry heavy burdens,
and I will give you rest. Take my yoke upon you. Let me teach you, because
I am humble and gentle at heart, and you will find rest for your souls.
For my yoke is easy to bear, and the burden I give you is light.'"
Matthew 11:28-30

PRAYER:

Dear Lord, You promise never to leave me alone nor to abandon me in my time of need. I thank you for your promises. Amen.

AFFIRMATION:

I will come unto you, oh Lord, and I will receive rest.

DAY 241: *Promise*

"And the same God who takes care of me will supply all your needs from His glorious riches, which have been given to us in Christ Jesus."
Philippians 4:19

PRAYER:

Heavenly Father, I am thankful for You being a faithful Father. You have supplied all of my needs. I can depend on my Lord. You always come through. You are indeed a faithful God. Thank You for every blessing. In Jesus' Name, Amen.

AFFIRMATION:

Thank You, Lord, for supplying all my needs.

DAY 242: *Promise*

"When I think of all this, I fall to my knees and pray to the Father,
the Creator of everything in Heaven and on earth. I pray that from His glorious,
unlimited resources He will empower you with inner strength through His Spirit."
Ephesians 3:14-16

PRAYER:
Dear God, Please give me the strength to face the day and to see the many blessings that it contains. Help me to trust in Your plan and to know that You are with me every step of the way. Please fill me with Your strength and peace, and give me wisdom to make good decisions. I offer my struggles to You and ask that You carry me through, in Jesus' Name, Amen.

AFFIRMATION:
Thank You for giving me power and strength in my weakness.

DAY 243: *Promise*

"Children, obey your parents, because you belong to the Lord, for this is the right thing to do. 'Honor your father and mother.' This is the first commandment with a promise, if you honor your father and mother, 'things will go well for you, and you will have a long life on the earth.'"

Ephesians 6:1-3

PRAYER:

Dear Lord, You are faithful. I thank You for every promise. I believe Your Word is true, and that You will guard my heart and mind in Christ Jesus as I surrender my heart to You. In Jesus' Name, Amen.

AFFIRMATION:

I will honor my father and mother all of the days of my life. God promised me a long life on the earth.

DAY 244: *Promise*

"And we know that God causes everything to work together for the good of those who love God and are called according to His purpose for them."

Romans 8:28

PRAYER:

Dear Lord, You promise to work all things together for the good of those who love you. No matter what troubles I face, You are working things out for my good. Thank You for being a sovereign God. Amen.

AFFIRMATION:

Be strong and courageous! Do not be afraid or discouraged. For the Lord your God is with you wherever you go.

DAY 245: *Promise*

"Keep on asking, and you will receive what you ask for. Keep on seeking, and you will find. Keep on knocking, and the door will be opened to you."
Matthew 7:7

PRAYER:
Dear Lord, You promise if I ask, I will receive. If I seek, I will find, and if I knock on the door, it will open for me. I believe the spoken Word of the Lord, Amen.

AFFIRMATION:
I will delight myself in Your Word and will not forget it.

WEEK 36: *Peace*

DAY 246: *Peace*

"For the Kingdom of God is not a matter of what we eat or drink, but of living a life of goodness and peace and joy in the Holy Spirit."

Romans 14:17

PRAYER:

Dear Lord, my desire is to live a peaceful life. I'm choosing to fix my eyes on You. I am claiming and declaring Your promises of peace and strength over my life. I need the strength and peace that only You can give. In Jesus' Name, Amen.

AFFIRMATION:

I am at peace with myself and everything that surrounds me.

DAY 247: *Peace*

"God blesses those who work for peace, for they will be called the children of God."
Matthew 5:9

PRAYER:
Dear Lord, You bless those who work for peace. Lord, You have called us to live in light of eternity during every hour of the day and night. Lord, make me a peacemaker in Jesus' Name, Amen.

AFFIRMATION:
I am a peaceful warrior.

DAY 248: *Peace*

"But the Holy Spirit produces this kind of fruit in our lives:
love, joy, peace, patience, kindness, goodness, faithfulness, gentleness,
and self-control. There is no law against these things."
Galatians 5:22-23

PRAYER:

Dear Lord, I thank You for being my peace. Help me in every situation, with thanksgiving, to present my requests to You. I praise You regardless of my circumstances. Give me true peace of mind through Christ. In Jesus' Name, Amen.

AFFIRMATION:

Peace exists within me and around me.

DAY 249: *Peace*

"Do all that you can to live in peace with everyone."

Romans 12:18

PRAYER:

Lord, You are my peace. Help me to live in peace everywhere I go. Help me trust and rest in You at all times. I joyfully receive Your peace, in Jesus' Name, Amen.

AFFIRMATION:

I am a peacemaker.

DAY 250: *Peace*

"I am leaving you with a gift: peace of mind and heart. And the peace I give is a gift the world cannot give. So don't be troubled or afraid."
John 14:27

PRAYER:
Dear Lord, make me an instrument of your peace. I am claiming and declaring your promises for blessings of peace. I really need the strength and peace that only You can give. In Jesus' Name, I pray. Amen.

AFFIRMATION:
I have inner peace and happiness.

DAY 251: *Peace*

"I have told you all this so that you may have peace in me. Here on earth you will have many trials and sorrows. But take heart, because I have overcome the world."

John 16:33

PRAYER:

Dear God, thank you for being our peace. You are our Protector. Guide our steps in the way of peace. Even though I walk through the darkest valley, I will fear no evil, for You are with me. Your rod and staff comfort me. In Jesus' Name, Amen.

AFFIRMATION:

My peace will not be interrupted.

DAY 252: *Peace*

"Thou wilt keep him in perfect peace whose mind is stayed on Thee: because he trusted in Thee."

Isaiah 26:3

PRAYER:

Heavenly Father, I put my trust in You today. Help me to keep my mind on You. For You are my peace. In Jesus' Name, I pray. Amen.

AFFIRMATION:

Nothing can disrupt my peace in Jesus' Name.

WEEK 37: *Evil*

DAY 253: *Evil*

"Don't let evil conquer you, but conquer evil by doing good."

Romans 12:21

PRAYER:

Dear Lord, You have given me the power to overcome evil. I will conquer evil by doing good. You are faithful Lord, and I trust You. Amen.

AFFIRMATION:

I will stay away from evil paths.

DAY 254: *Evil*

"All who do evil hate the light and refuse to go near it for fear their sins will be exposed."
John 3:20

PRAYER:
Dear Lord, the name of the Lord is a fortified tower; the righteous run to it and are safe. Lord, help me to represent the Kingdom being a beacon of light. In Jesus' Name, Amen.

AFFIRMATION:
I am radiant.

DAY 255: *Evil*

"Don't repay evil for evil. Don't retaliate with insults when people insult you. Instead, pay them back with a blessing. That is what God has called you to do, and He will grant you His blessing."
1 Peter 3:9

PRAYER:
Our Father, in the name of Jesus, help me to keep my mind on You. Lord, protect me from all evil. Teach me Your ways never to render evil for evil. I will be a blessing to them, in Jesus' Name, Amen.

AFFIRMATION:
I will bless all that repaid me with evil.

DAY 256: *Evil*

"Don't be impressed with your own wisdom. Instead, fear the Lord and turn away from evil."

Proverbs 3:7

PRAYER:

Dear Lord, I thank You for making a way of escape. I will put my trust in the all-knowing God that is full of wisdom. I will fear the Lord and turn away from evil, in Jesus' Name, Amen.

AFFIRMATION:

I will use wisdom and turn away from evil.

DAY 257: *Evil*

"Stay away from every kind of evil."
1 Thessalonians 5:22

PRAYER:
Dear Lord, You are a shield around me. I will fear no evil, for You watch over me. You defend and deliver me. I will put my trust in You every day. Thank You, Lord, for being my shield. In Jesus' Name, Amen.

AFFIRMATION:
I choose to do good instead of evil.

DAY 258: *Evil*

"For the wicked will be destroyed, but those who trust in the Lord will possess the land."

Psalm 37:9

PRAYER:

Dear Lord, some trust in chariots, and some in horses, but we will trust in the name of the Lord our God. Your goodness and mercy surround us daily, so we will not fear whatever might come against us. In Jesus' Name, Amen.

AFFIRMATION:

Father, lead us out of temptation and deliver us from evil.

DAY 259: *Evil*

"What sorrow for those to say that evil is good and good is evil,
that dark is light and light is dark, that bitter is sweet and sweet is bitter."
Isaiah 5:20

PRAYER:

Our Father who art in Heaven, hallowed be Thy name. Thy Kingdom come, Thy will be done, on earth as it is in Heaven. Father, You have given us Jesus. We know that Jesus is the light of this world. We choose to do good over evil in Jesus' Name, Amen.

AFFIRMATION:

I will conquer evil by doing good.

WEEK 38: *Prayer*

DAY 260: *Prayer*

"Our Father in Heaven, may Your name be kept holy. May Your Kingdom come soon. May Your will be done on earth, as it is in Heaven. Give us today the food we need, and forgive us our sins, as we have forgiven those who sin against us. And don't let us yield to temptation, but rescue us from the evil one."

Matthew 6:9-13

PRAYER:

Dear God, You are holy and sovereign. I am thankful for all that You do. The Lord our God is supreme over all gods and over all powers. You are great and mighty. I will praise You forever in Jesus' Mighty Name. Amen.

AFFIRMATION:

God's will be done in the earth.

DAY 261: *Prayer*

"Don't worry about anything; instead, pray about everything.
Tell God what you need, and thank Him for all He has done. Then you
will experience God's peace, which exceeds anything we can understand.
His peace will guard your hearts and minds as you live in Christ Jesus."
Philippians 4:6-7

PRAYER:

Dear Lord, Your Word says that I should not worry. Lift the full weight of worry from my shoulders. Help me to cast all my cares on You. Increase my ability to trust Your faithfulness and Your sovereign plan for my life. In Jesus' Name, Amen.

AFFIRMATION:

The Spirit of the Lord speaks through me. His Word is upon my tongue.

DAY 262: *Prayer*

"Confess your sins to each other and pray for each other so that you may be healed. The earnest prayer of a righteous person has great power and produces wonderful results."
James 5:16

PRAYER:

Dear Lord, thank You for Your instructions. I am grateful that You hear my prayers. You have declared that the earnest prayer of a righteous person has great power and produces wonderful results. I thank You for always hearing my prayer. Amen.

AFFIRMATION:

I am forgiven and free from sin and guilt.

DAY 263: *Prayer*

"Always be joyful. Never stop praying. Be thankful in all circumstances. For this is God's will for you who belong to Christ Jesus."
1 Thessalonians 5:16-18

PRAYER:

Dear Lord, I thank You for Your loving kindness. I have so many things to be thankful for. The joy of the Lord is my strength. Thank You Lord for being our strength when we are weak. Lord, You are worthy of all praise, blessing, honor, and glory. In Jesus' Name, Amen.

AFFIRMATION:

God's glory will be revealed through my life.

DAY 264: *Prayer*

"Put on salvation as your helmet, and take the sword of the Spirit, which is the Word of God. Pray in the Spirit at all times and on every occasion. Stay alert and be persistent in your prayers for all believers everywhere."

Ephesians 6:17-18

PRAYER:

Dear Lord, I am thankful for the armor You have provided. I put on the belt of truth, the breastplate of righteousness, the shoes of peace, and the helmet of salvation. I lift up the shield of faith against all the fiery darts of the enemy, and I take in my hand the Word of God as the sword of the Spirit. I put on this armor every day. I trust and depend on You. In Jesus' Name, I pray. Amen.

AFFIRMATION:

I am who God says I am.

DAY 265: *Prayer*

"And we are confident that He hears us whenever we ask for anything that pleases Him. And since we know He hears us when we make our requests, we also know that He will give us what we ask for."

1 John 5:14-15

PRAYER:

Dear Lord, it is in confidence that I approach you. I pray in confidence that You will grant my request. May I be confident in Your promise and remain faithful to You, even in the hard times. I will wait patiently on You, dear Lord. In Jesus' Name, Amen.

AFFIRMATION:

The Lord of my life walks with me.

DAY 266: *Prayer*

"When you pray, don't be like the hypocrites who love to pray publicly on street corners and in the synagogues where everyone can see them. I tell you the truth, that is all the reward they will ever get. But when you pray, go away by yourself, shut the door behind you, and pray to your Father in private. Then your Father, who sees everything, will reward you. When you pray, don't babble on and on as the Gentiles do. They think their prayers are answered merely by repeating their words again and again. Don't be like them, for your Father knows exactly what you need even before you ask Him!"

Matthew 6:5-8

PRAYER:

Dear Lord, Remind me each morning of Your constant love, for I put my trust in You. Teach me to do Your will. Be good to me, and guide me on a safe path. In Jesus' Name, I pray. Amen.

AFFIRMATION:

Because of my covenant walk with God, He will make me to prosper.

WEEK 39: *Trouble*

DAY 267: *Trouble*

"When you go through deep waters, I will be with you. When you go through rivers of difficulty, you will not drown. When you walk through the fire of oppression, you will not be burned up; the flames will not consume you.

Isaiah 43:2

PRAYER:

Dear Jesus, please watch over me during these difficult situations. Be my source of strength. I glorify you during these times because this is Your perfect will in my life. Amen.

AFFIRMATION:

I have the ability to recover from difficulties.

DAY 268: *Trouble*

"Don't let your hearts be troubled. Trust in God, and trust also in me."
John 14:1

PRAYER:
Dear Jesus, I believe every word that You said. I forgive those who hurt me intentionally. I release it and give it to You. I will allow You to heal my heart. Lord, You are my healer. Heal me where there is pain or discomfort. I trust the healing process in Jesus' Name, Amen.

AFFIRMATION:
I forgive those who have hurt me.

DAY 269: *Trouble*

"God blesses those who mourn, for they will be comforted."
Matthew 5:4

PRAYER:
Dear Jesus, I am strong. I can make it. I will win. I refuse to lose in life. I am destined to win. Lord, nothing is too difficult for You. The Lord is my Shepherd; I have all that I need. I am mourning today. My God will see me through this challenging time. Amen.

AFFIRMATION:
I can get through anything with Christ on my side.

DAY 270: *Trouble*

"I will lift up mine eyes unto the hills from whence cometh my help. My help cometh from the Lord, which made heaven and earth."

Psalm 121:1-2

PRAYER:

Dear Jesus, You are the way, the truth, and the life. I know You are faithful to provide for me. You are all that I need, and all wisdom flows from You. When I call on You, Lord, You are faithful to answer. Jesus, You are my help. I will always run to You. In Jesus' Name, Amen.

AFFIRMATION:

My ability to conquer challenges is limitless, my potential to succeed is infinite.

DAY 271: *Trouble*

"The Lord is good, a strong refuge when trouble comes. He is close to those who trust in Him."

Nahum 1:7

PRAYER:

Dear Lord, You are my refuge. I run to You and You cover me. You will uphold and protect me. I can trust You, Lord, that You will come through for me. Lord, help me to rely on You. Through Jesus Christ, our Lord, Amen.

AFFIRMATION:

Everyday I become more confident, powerful, and successful.

DAY 272: *Trouble*

"We are pressed on every side by troubles, but we are not crushed. We are perplexed, but not driven to despair. We are hunted down, but never abandoned by God. We get knocked down, but we are not destroyed."

2 Corinthians 4:8-9

PRAYER:

Dear Jesus, help me. I need Your help in spite of weakness, falls, and shortcomings of every kind. Jesus, please help me and never forsake me. Oh Lord, You are my refuge and strength. You are my present help in the time of need. I thank You and give You praise, Amen.

AFFIRMATION:

I will face challenges, but they are impermanent, and I have the strength to overcome.

DAY 273: *Trouble*

"God is our refuge and strength, always ready to help in times of trouble."
Psalm 46:1

PRAYER:

Oh God, I thank You for being there for me. You are my shield and buckler. When I am vulnerable, You are my refuge. When I cry for help, You will answer. I can't see a way out, but You can make a way. Through Jesus Christ, our Lord, Amen.

AFFIRMATION:

My mission in life is not merely to survive, but to thrive. God is with me.

WEEK 40: *Treasures*

DAY 274: *Treasures*

"A good person produces good things from the treasury of a good heart, and an evil person produces evil things from the treasury of an evil heart."
Matthew 12:35

PRAYER:
Dear Lord, I pray that I will produce good things from the treasury of a good heart. Help me, Lord, to secure a spiritual treasure which is eternal in you. Spiritual treasures bring joy, blessings, success, and even wealth, so my prayer is Lord help me to secure a spiritual treasure in You. In Jesus' Name, Amen.

AFFIRMATION:
I am self-assured.

DAY 275: *Treasures*

"The wise have wealth and luxury, but fools spend whatever they get. Whoever pursues righteousness and unfailing love will find life, righteousness, and honor."

Proverbs 21:20-21

PRAYER:

Dear Lord, teach me to store my treasures in heaven rather than here on earth. Help me to see those who need my help, that in my heart there is no greed, but generosity, a desire to help others. I also pray that I will not fail your Kingdom. It is in the name of Jesus, I pray. Amen.

AFFIRMATION:

There is a time to spend and also a time to save.

DAY 276: *Treasures*

"No one can serve two masters. For you will hate one and love the other; you will be devoted to one and despise the other. You cannot serve God and be enslaved to money."

Matthew 6:24

PRAYER:

Dear Lord, today we acknowledge You for who You are. You are the sovereign Lord. You have been with us from the beginning. We cannot serve two masters. Today, our confession is that we serve the living God. Jesus is Lord over our lives. Jesus is our Savior and we treasure Him. This is our prayer in Jesus' Name, Amen.

AFFIRMATION:

I chose to serve the only wise God. His name is Jesus.

DAY 277: *Treasures*

"The Kingdom of Heaven is like a treasure that a man discovered hidden in a field. In his excitement, he hid it again and sold everything he owned to get enough money to buy the field."

Matthew 13:44

PRAYER:

Dear Lord, I thank You, Lord, for today, because I am secured in You. You are the treasure that I seek -- my great reward. You sustain me by Your grace and protect me by Your great power. You are my greatest treasure, in Jesus' Name, Amen.

AFFIRMATION:

What God has for me, it is for me.

DAY 278: *Treasures*

"Wherever your treasure is, there the desires of your heart will also be."

Matthew 6:21

PRAYER:

Dear Lord, I thank You for the greatest treasure that we have, the treasures of journeying life with You. Everything we own belongs to You. We declare You are the treasure we seek. You are our all in all. In Jesus' Name, I pray. Amen.

AFFIRMATION:

I am worthy of love, happiness, and success.

DAY 279: *Treasures*

"Don't store up treasures here on earth, where moths eat them and rust destroys them, and where thieves break in and steal. Store your treasures in heaven, where moths and rust cannot destroy, and thieves do not break and steal. Wherever your treasure is, there the desires of your heart will also be."

Matthew 6:19-21

PRAYER:

Dear Lord, thank You for giving me a new way of thinking. I know that I can store my treasures in heaven, where moths and rust cannot destroy, and thieves do not break and steal. Oh Lord, You are my Greatest Treasure, in Jesus' Name, I pray. Amen.

AFFIRMATION:

I choose not to store my treasures on earth, but to store my treasures in heaven.

DAY 280: *Treasures*

"And I will give you treasures hidden in the darkness - secret riches. I will do this so you may know that I am the Lord, the God of Israel, the One who calls you by name."

Isaiah 45:3

PRAYER:

Dear Lord, I thank You for the promises of the Lord. That you will give me hidden treasures, secret riches. You provide for me by Your mercy and love me always by Your faithfulness. Great are You, Lord, and greatly to be praised. In Jesus' Name, Amen.

AFFIRMATION:

I am abundant.

WEEK 41: *Friends*

DAY 281: *Friends*

"The godly give good advice to their friends; the wicked lead them astray."

Proverbs 12:26

PRAYER:

Dear Lord, I lift up my friends who are mourning a loved one. I ask that You will bring them comfort in the midst of this life-shaking event. Thank You for being the God of all comfort, the One who holds us in Your hand. I give You praise, in Jesus' Name, Amen.

AFFIRMATION:

I am a true friend and loyal to the end.

DAY 282: *Friends*

"One should be kind to a fainting friend, but you accuse me without any fear of the Almighty."
Job 6:14

PRAYER:
Dear Lord, teach us to show ourselves to be friendly. Friends should be kind to one another. We pray that our friends will open their hearts to what You have to offer them in terms of healing, mercy, love, and guidance. In Jesus' Name, Amen.

AFFIRMATION:
We will show others how to be a friend.

DAY 283: *Friends*

"Do to others as you would like them to do to you."

Luke 6:31

PRAYER:

Our Father, today we are asking for Your help. Teach us "in everything, do to others what you would have them do to you". This is our duty to do to others the way we want to be treated. Thank You for the true friends that You have given me, in Jesus' Name, Amen.

AFFIRMATION:

We will treat others the way we want to be treated.

DAY 284: *Friends*

"Dear friends, since God loved us that much, we surely ought to love each other."

1 John 4:11

PRAYER:

Dear Lord, thank You so much for my friends and the spiritual impact they have made in my life. I pray for nothing but thanksgiving for them and that our friendship will only continue to blossom. I pray this in Jesus' Name, Amen.

AFFIRMATION:

We will remember to give time to our friends.

DAY 285: *Friends*

"A friend is always loyal and a brother is born to help in time of need."

Proverbs 17:17

PRAYER:

Dear Lord, I give thanks for You sending me loyal friends. Teach me how to be loyal to my friends as well. I pray for Your guidance. Thank You for answering my prayer. In Jesus' Name, I pray. Amen.

AFFIRMATION:

My friends and I encourage one another in all our efforts.

DAY 286: *Friends*

"There is no greater love than to lay down one's life for one's friends."
John 15:13

PRAYER:

Dear Lord, thank You for the amazing love You have shown us. There is no greater love than to lay down one's life for one's friends. Thank You, Jesus, that we have no greater friend than You. You gave your perfect life to redeem ours. May we see that it is only the pursuit of You that will give our lives meaning. In Jesus' Name, I pray. Amen.

AFFIRMATION:

Jesus is a True Friend.

DAY 287: *Friends*

"When Job prayed for his friends, the Lord restored his fortunes. In fact, the Lord gave him twice as much as before!"
Job 42:10

PRAYER:

Dear Lord, teach us how to pray for our friends. Sometimes our friends are not friendly. We are reminded that Job prayed for his friends and the Lord restored him. Today, we pray for our friends that despitefully use us. We bless them today in Jesus' Name. Amen.

AFFIRMATION:

We desire to be sensitive to the needs of others.

WEEK 42: *Children*

DAY 288: *Children*

"Children, always obey your parents, for this pleases the Lord."
Colossians 3:20

PRAYER:
Dear Lord, please bless our children. Protect our children from the negative pressures placed upon them by their peers. Protect them wherever they go. Help them make the right choices about things they should and shouldn't do. We pray for our children to obey their parents for this pleases the Lord. Amen.

AFFIRMATION:
Our children will obey their parents for this pleases the Lord.

DAY 289: *Children*

"Train up a child in the way he should go, and when he is old he will not depart from it."

Proverbs 22:6

PRAYER:

Dear Lord, today we pray that our children would walk close to You. We pray that they would have the hearts of a servant. Lord, save our children from unnecessary pain. Let them have a hunger for righteousness. Our children would become people of great wisdom in Jesus' Name. Amen.

AFFIRMATION:

Our children are our future and they shall lead the way.

DAY 290: *Children*

"I could have no greater joy than to hear that my children are following the truth."

3 John 1:4

PRAYER:

Dear Lord, thank You for our youth. We pray that our youth are following Jesus. Our prayer is that they will know the truth that Jesus is our Lord. Jesus is the only begotten son of God. We thank You, Lord, for our children shall know the truth. In Jesus' Name, Amen.

AFFIRMATION:

The Truth shall set you free.

DAY 291: *Children*

"Don't let anyone think less of you because you are young. Be an example to all believers in what you say, in the way you live, in your love, your faith, and your purity."
1 Timothy 4:12

PRAYER:
Dear Lord, I pray that our children will represent Your Kingdom well in the earth. Our children are the salt of the earth. They will show love and kindness everywhere they go. Our children are the light of this world, unable to be hidden. We give You praise for our children in Jesus' Name. Amen.

AFFIRMATION:
Our children will operate in the fruit of the spirit.

DAY 292: *Children*

"Beware that you don't look down on any of these little ones. For I tell you that in heaven their angels are always in the presence of my heavenly Father."
Matthew 18:10

PRAYER:
Dear Father, create in our children a pure heart, and renew a steadfast spirit within them. Help our children to know Your word and to grow in faith each day. I pray that our children will come to understand the extent of Your love. I pray that they will be filled up with You from morning till night. In Jesus' Name, Amen.

AFFIRMATION:
I declare that children are a gift from the Lord. They are a reward from Him.

DAY 293: *Children*

"Children are a gift from the Lord; they are a reward from Him."

Psalm 127:3

PRAYER:

Dear Lord, thank You for our children. Our children are a gift from the Lord. Help them to become who You created them to be. We believe that our children are great leaders. They will fulfill destiny in Jesus' Holy Name. Amen.

AFFIRMATION:

Our children will represent God with righteousness.

DAY 294: *Children*

"I will teach all Your children, and they will enjoy great peace."
Isaiah 54:13

PRAYER:

Our Father, who art in Heaven, hallowed be Thy name; Thy Kingdom come, Thy will be done, on earth as it is in Heaven. Thank you for Your Son Jesus being our teacher. He demonstrated how we should love the children. He taught us to train up a child in the way he should go; and when he is old, he will not depart from it. Lord, our children will enjoy great peace in Jesus' Name, Amen.

AFFIRMATION:

Our children will do great exploits for the Kingdom of God.

WEEK 43: *Evidence*

DAY 295: *Evidence*

"If your brother or sister sins, go and point out their fault, just between the two of you. If they listen to you, you have won them over. But if they will not listen, take one or two others along, so that 'every matter may be established by the testimony of two or three witnesses'."
Matthew 18:15-16

PRAYER:
Dear Lord, thank You for showing us how we should live. Your desire is for us to live peacefully with one another. Thank You, Lord, that I can see Your face and live for You with peace and joy. In Jesus' Name, Amen.

AFFIRMATION:
The more I learn, the more I can accomplish.

DAY 296: *Evidence*

"This is the third time I am coming to visit you, and as the scripture says,
'the facts of every case must be established by the testimony of two or three witnesses'."
2 Corinthians 13:1

PRAYER:

Dear Lord, help me to always speak the truth in love and to live a life of truthfulness. Help me to rely on Your strength to tell the truth in every situation. May your words and actions reflect your truth and bring you glory in Jesus' Name. Amen.

AFFIRMATION:

The evidence I shall give, shall be the truth, the whole truth, and nothing but the truth.

DAY 297: *Evidence*

"'Which ones?' The man asked. And Jesus replied, 'You must not murder. You must not commit adultery. You must not steal. You must not testify falsely.'"
Matthew 19:18

PRAYER:

Dear Lord, I need Your help right now. I pray that I will not sin against You. Lord, help me to live by Your word and to keep Your commandments. Please strengthen my faith with solid evidence so that I may truly live for Jesus.

AFFIRMATION:

We must obey God's commandments and keep His words.

DAY 298: *Evidence*

"So faith comes from hearing, that is, hearing the good news of Christ."
Romans 10:17

PRAYER:
Dear Lord, I welcome faith. No matter what happens, my faith is unshakeable. I believe the Word of God. Through my faith, I can achieve the impossible. The evidence of my faith is to hear the Word of the Lord. Amen.

AFFIRMATION:
I have the freedom and power to create the life I desire.

DAY 299: *Evidence*

"You must not testify falsely against your neighbor."
Exodus 20:16

PRAYER:
Dear God, Your Word is true. We have been warned not to testify falsely against our neighbor. So it's our duty and responsibility to be truthful at all times. Help us to be mindful of telling the truth. You told us to know the truth, and the truth will set you free. Amen.

AFFIRMATION:
It is my responsibility to speak the truth at all times.

DAY 300: *Evidence*

"Work at living in peace with everyone, and work at living a holy life, for those who are not holy will not see the Lord."
Hebrews 12:14

PRAYER:

Dear Lord, You are my peace. I am thankful for the peace that I have experienced in You. I stop right now to give You thanks. Above all, thank You for Your Son, for what He did for me. I am reminded of Your goodness. In Jesus' Name, I pray. Amen.

AFFIRMATION:

I choose to be kind to everyone and to love unconditionally.

DAY 301: *Evidence*

"All scripture is inspired by God and is useful to teach us
what is true and to make us realize what is wrong in our lives.
It corrects us when we are wrong and teaches us to do what is right."
2 Timothy 3:16

PRAYER:
Heavenly Father, You are our evidence by the very gift of the Bible as God's revelation of Himself to man. You have made it plain that You exist. Our mission is to make You known by proclaiming Christ. Through prayer, we find evidence of God's existence. If we make a habit of prayer in our life, the evidence of God's existence reveals itself. We thank You, Lord, for the evidence that You exist. In Jesus' Name, Amen.

AFFIRMATION:
The Word of God is my evidence!

WEEK 44: *Flowers*

DAY 302: *Flowers*

"Now learn a lesson from the fig tree. When its branches bud and its leaves begin to sprout, you know that summer is near. In the same way, when you see all these things, you can know His return is very near, right at the door."

Matthew 24:32-33

PRAYER:

Heavenly Father, thank You for the signs that have given to us, Your children. Help us to know the seasons. Teach us Your ways that no matter what winds blow, that we are anchored in You. We will be all that You will have us to be. In Jesus' Name, Amen.

AFFIRMATION:

Flowers are spiritual messengers.

DAY 303: *Flowers*

"Your cheeks are like rosy pomegranates behind your veil."

Song of Solomon 6:7

PRAYER:

Dear Lord, allow me to blossom like a beautiful flower. My cheeks are like rosy pomegranates. My smile is bright as sunshine. My love for You, Lord, is everlasting. In Jesus' Name, Amen.

AFFIRMATION:

You shall blossom like a beautiful flower.

DAY 304: *Flowers*

"I will be to Israel like a refreshing dew from heaven. Israel will blossom like the lily; it will send roots deep into the soil like the cedars in Lebanon. Its branches will spread out like beautiful olive trees, as fragrant as the cedars of Lebanon."
Hosea 14:5-6

PRAYER:
Dear Lord, I am Your creation. Let my fragrance be as the cedars of Lebanon. Allow me to spread love and happiness. I want others to receive Your peace and joy. In Jesus' Name, Amen.

AFFIRMATION:
Flowers are God's creation.

DAY 305: *Flowers*

"Where once there were thorns, cypress trees will grow.
Where nettles grew, myrtles will sprout up. These events will bring great honor
to the Lord's name; they will be an everlasting sign of His power and love."
Isaiah 55:13

PRAYER:

Our Father, Thank You for Your Son Jesus. We need Him now. We know His name is all-powerful. There is no other name that men can be saved. Jesus is everlasting to everlasting. His name is great and greatly to be praised. Amen.

AFFIRMATION:

I am a beautiful flower, and I will fill the world with my sweet fragrance.

DAY 306: *Flowers*

"Look at the lilies and how they grow. They don't work or make their clothing, yet Solomon in all his glory was not dressed as beautifully as they are."

Luke 12:27

PRAYER:

Dear Lord, You made the lilies of the field to grow. You have provided everything we need as well. Our trust is in You, Lord. You are Our Creator. Help us, Lord, to trust in the providence of God. In Jesus' Name, Amen.

AFFIRMATION:

A flower radiates.

DAY 307: *Flowers*

"I am the rose of Sharon, and the lily of the valleys."

Song of Solomon 2:1

PRAYER:

Heavenly Father, We praise Your name. Your name is Wonderful. You are the Rose of Sharon and the Lily of the Valley. The Bright and Morning Star. Emmanuel, You are with us. We say thank you, in Jesus' Mighty Name, Amen.

AFFIRMATION:

The spiritual dimension of nature can only be revealed through the eyes of a believer.

DAY 308: *Flowers*

"Yes, there will be an abundance of flowers and singing and joy.
The desert will become as green as the mountain of Lebanon, as lovely as Mount Carmel
or the plain of Sharon. There the Lord will display His glory, the splendor of our God."
Isaiah 35:2

PRAYER:

Dear Lord, thank You for displaying Your glory and splendor. There will be an abundance of Your beauty. The Kingdom of God is full of flowers. Let my flowers blossom in the name of Jesus. Amen.

AFFIRMATION:

I declare that I will blossom like a flower garden.

WEEK 45: *Mercy*

DAY 309: *Mercy*

"He shows mercy from generation to generation to all who fear Him."

Luke 1:50

PRAYER:

Heavenly Father, Thank You for being a merciful God. You show mercy from generation to generation. You give us new mercies every day. In Jesus' Name, I pray. Amen

AFFIRMATION:

My God is merciful and kind.

DAY 310: *Mercy*

"Let us, therefore, come boldly unto the throne of grace,
that we may obtain mercy, and find grace to help in time of need."
Hebrews 4:16

PRAYER:

Heavenly Father, thank You for Your grace and mercy. Lord, I pray for your love and mercy to complete me and make me whole. Pour upon me your grace and strength to stand in faith even in trying times. In Jesus' Name, Amen.

AFFIRMATION:

I accept the mercy, grace, and peace of Christ.

DAY 311: *Mercy*

"'I'm in a desperate situation!' David replied to God. 'But let us fall into the hands of the Lord, for His mercy is great. Do not let me fall into human hands.'"

2 Samuel 24:14

PRAYER:

Dear Lord, I thank You that You are the God of all mercy. Let Your mercy surround me. Do not let me fall into human hands. But let us fall into the hands of the Lord, for His mercy is great. In Jesus' name, Amen.

AFFIRMATION:

I am receiving infinite grace and mercy now and always.

DAY 312: *Mercy*

"The faithful love of the Lord never ends! His mercies never cease. Great is His faithfulness; His mercies begin afresh each morning."
Lamentations 3:22-23

PRAYER:
Heavenly Father, I thank You for Your loving kindness. You give us new mercies every day. Great is Your faithfulness. The Lord is good to all, and His mercy is over all that He has made. I give You praise in Jesus' Name. Amen.

AFFIRMATION:
My heart is full of mercy.

DAY 313: *Mercy*

"For He saith to Moses, 'I will have mercy on whom I will have mercy, and I will have compassion on whom I will have compassion'."

Romans 9:15,

PRAYER:

Heavenly Father, You are the God of all mercy. I thank You for Your loving kindness and compassion. I thank You for Your mercy, for it will never be exhausted. In Jesus' Name, Amen.

AFFIRMATION:

I declare that God's mercies are new every morning.

DAY 314: *Mercy*

"God blesses those who are merciful, for they will be shown mercy."

Matthew 5:7

PRAYER:

Heavenly Father, help us to be merciful and kind. Help us to show love and mercy to one another. Your Son, Jesus, was a perfect example to us. He showed mercy to all. We thank You Lord, in Jesus' Name, Amen.

AFFIRMATION:

I declare that I will sow mercy.

DAY 315: *Mercy*

"But the Lord our God is merciful and forgiving, even though we have rebelled against Him."
Daniel 9:9

PRAYER:

Dear Lord, Our God is merciful and forgiving. Teach us how to be merciful and forgiving as well. We are Your children. We want to represent You well. So thank You, Lord, for being a merciful God. In Jesus' Name, Amen.

AFFIRMATION:

Mercy is Christlike, and it's powerful.

WEEK 46: *Light*

DAY 316: *Light*

"And the city had no need of the sun, neither of the moon, to shine in it: for the glory of God did lighten it, and the Lamb is the light thereof."
Revelation 21: 23

PRAYER:
Heavenly Father, the city had no need of the sun, neither of the moon, to shine in it. God did lighten it, and we are forever grateful. Help us to be a light that shines, the people around will see our glow in Jesus' Name, Amen.

AFFIRMATION:
I am clothed in the righteousness of Christ.

DAY 317: *Light*

"Arise, shine, for thy light is come, and the glory of the Lord is risen upon thee."
Isaiah 60:1

PRAYER:

Dear Father, thank You for being the light that we all need. Help us to be sensitive to the needs of others. Help us to be the light they need during their darkest days. We want to be intentional about helping others. To be the light, we must know the Light, and the light is found in Jesus. Amen.

AFFIRMATION:

I am clothed with strength and dignity.

DAY 318: *Light*

"Then spake Jesus again unto them, saying, 'I am the light of the world: he that followeth me shall not walk in darkness, but shall have the light of life.'"

John 8:12

PRAYER:

Our Father, shine your light on my path. In You, there is no darkness. My decision is final. I decided to follow Jesus. Help me to stay on that path that You have for me. In the mighty Name of Jesus, Amen.

AFFIRMATION:

I am a follower of Christ Jesus.

DAY 319: *Light*

"The Lord is my light and my salvation, so why should I be afraid?
The Lord is my fortress, protecting me from danger, so why should I tremble?
Psalm 27:1

PRAYER:

Dear Heavenly Father, I thank You that You are light, and in You is no darkness at all. I thank You that You see my situation, and You know my situation. I will not tremble. Thank You, Father God. I love You, and I give You all the glory. In Jesus' Name, Amen.

AFFIRMATION:

I am a being of Light.

DAY 320: *Light*

"For you are all children of the Light and of the day. We don't belong to darkness and night." 1 Thessalonians 5:5

PRAYER:

Dear Lord, allow me to be a light in this dark and gloomy world. May I be a blessing to others. Give me opportunities to shine whether in the workplace, my family, my community, or among friends. You are the light of the world shining through me, in Jesus' Name, Amen.

AFFIRMATION:

I am God's masterpiece.

DAY 321: *Light*

"Light is sweet; how pleasant to see a new day dawning."

Ecclesiastes 11:7

PRAYER:

Dear Lord, You are the light of the world. Our hope is in You. May Your light and love blaze in us. Make us to walk as children of light in all goodness and righteousness, that we may have no fellowship with the unfruitful works of darkness, through Jesus Christ our Lord. Amen.

AFFIRMATION:

Jesus is a good and perfect gift to us from God the Father.

DAY 322: *Light*

"The Word is a lamp unto my feet, and a light unto my path."
Psalm 119:105

PRAYER:

Dear Lord, You are the giver of every good and perfect gift, who has made the light of Your truth shine in our hearts. Your Word is a lamp unto my feet. It will guide us in the right direction. May my light shine before those I encounter. In Jesus' Name, Amen.

AFFIRMATION:

I am the light of the world. I am a city on a hill that cannot be hidden.

WEEK 47: *Recovery*

Day 323: Recovery

"Then Jesus said,
'Come to me all of you who are weary and carry heavy burdens, and I will give you rest. Take my yoke upon you. Let me teach you,
because I am humble and gentle at heart, and you will find rest for your souls'."
Matthew 11:28-29

Prayer:
Dear Lord, I decided to give it all to You. This is too heavy for me to carry. I need rest. Lord, You are able to give me what I need. Letting go of what is troubling me is necessary. My future is ahead of me. I release it to You. In Jesus' Name, Amen.

Affirmation:
I choose to let go. I gave it all to God.

____
____
____
____
____
____
____
____
____
____

Day 324: Recovery

"For You are my hiding place; You protect me
from trouble. You surround me with songs of victory."
Psalm 32:7

Prayer:

Dear Lord, We run to You for safety. You are our hiding place. Sometimes, trouble is all around us. We must know that You are always with us. We thank You for being our shield and buckler. In Jesus' Name, Amen.

Affirmation:

There is no challenge too big for my God to handle.

Day 325: Recovery

"For all that is in the world, the lust of the flesh, and the lust of the eyes, and the pride of life, is not of the Father, but is of the world."
1 John 2:16

Prayer:
Dear Lord, the cross is in front of me. This world is behind me. I decided to make Jesus my choice. Taste and see that the Lord is good. Righteousness is a choice. Let my life represent the Lord well in all that I do. In Jesus' Holy Name, Amen.

Affirmation:
I am making improvements to my life to live Holy.

____

Day 326: Recovery

"The temptations in your life are no different from what others experience.
And God is faithful. He will not allow the temptation to be more than you can stand.
When you are tempted, He will show you a way out so that you can endure."
1 Corinthians 10:13

Prayer:
Heavenly Father, You are the great I Am. There were some times I wasn't pleased with myself. I fell into temptation. You are my deliverer, Lord. You made a way of escape for me. I will give You praise. In Jesus' Name, Amen.

Affirmation:
I'm recovering, in Jesus' Name.

____
____
____
____
____
____
____
____
____

Day 327: Recovery

"Oh Lord, if You heal me, I will be truly healed; if You save me, I will be truly saved. My praises are for You alone!"
Jeremiah 17:14

Prayer:
Dear Lord, this is the day that the Lord has made. I shall rejoice and be glad in it. I called on the Lord, and He answered me. Healing and deliverance belongs to me. I receive all that the Lord has for me. In Jesus' Name, Amen.

Affirmation:
Today, I choose to live in the moment.

Day 328: Recovery

"Come back to the place of safety, all you prisoners who still have hope!
I promise this very day that I will repay two blessings for each of your troubles."
Zachariah 9:12

Prayer:
Heavenly Father, my hope is in You. Thank You that in You all things are possible. I come before You today in need of Your healing hand. Thank You, Father, for healing me according to Your will and inspiring me to help others. In Jesus' Name, Amen.

Affirmation:
I am healed, and I forgive myself today.

____
____
____
____
____
____
____
____
____
____

Day 329: Recovery

"The spirit of the Lord is upon me, for He has anointed me to bring good news to the poor. He has sent me to proclaim that captives will
be released, that the blind will see, that the oppressed will be set free."
Luke 4:18

Prayer:
Dear Lord, many of us need healing. I need healing for past hurts, random physical pains that I allow to waylay my days. I receive my healing so that I may be whole and that I may be able to minister to others in a way that brings You glory. Allow me to show others Your healing power. In Jesus' Name, Amen.

Affirmation:
I am living as God intended.

____
____
____
____
____
____
____
____
____

Week 48:
Shine

Day 330: Shine

"Let your light so shine before men, that they may see your good works and glorify your Father who is in heaven."
Matthew 5:16

Prayer:
Dear Lord, I am determined to let my light so shine before men, that they may see Your good works. Keep me as the apple of Your eye, and hide me under the shadow of Your wings. Let Your Kingdom come, and Your will be done. In Jesus' Name, Amen.

Affirmation:

Today, I choose to shine brightly.

Day 331: Shine

"The way of the righteous is like the first gleam of dawn, which shines ever brighter until the full light of day."
Proverbs 4:18

Prayer:
Dear Lord, I am thankful for the gift of life. You are the light of the world. I desire to walk in the fullness of the light. My life should be a reflection of Your radiance. Dear Lord, keep me near the cross. In the Mighty Name of Jesus, I pray, Amen.

Affirmation:
Today, I direct my light to illuminate others.

Day 332: Shine

"And, behold, the angel of the Lord came upon him,
and a light shined in the prison, and he smote Peter on the side,
and raised
him up, saying, 'Arise up quickly'. And his chains fell off from his
hands."
Acts 12:7

Prayer:
Dear Father God, give me the strength to rise, and the light to shine bright. I pray that my light will not fade away. I will keep shining by the grace of God, in the Mighty Name of Jesus. Amen.

Affirmation:
Today, I recognize my inner light.

____
____
____
____
____
____
____
____
____
____

Day 333: Shine

"Do everything without complaining and arguing, so that no one can criticize you. Live clean, innocent lives as children of God, shining
like bright lights in a world full of crooked and perverse people."
Philippians 2:14-15

Prayer:
Dear God, I'm reminded of Your Word. You told us to put on the whole armor of God that we will be able to stand against the wiles of the devil. Lord, I pray against the powers of the wicked one. Lord, I come against any power trying to quench my fire and stop my shine. In Jesus' Name, Amen.

Affirmation:
I am radiant, and I shine my light for all to see.

Day 334: Shine

"Then the righteous will shine like the sun in their Father's Kingdom. Anyone with ears to hear should listen and understand!"
Matthew 13:43

Prayer:
Our Father, I thank You for being my God. My life is a representation of who You are. Make me a shining light. Let me stand before kings, and let my name be mentioned in high places, in the Name of Jesus, Amen.

Affirmation:
I declare that I am a powerful force and I shine everywhere I go.

Day 335: Shine

"Those who are wise will shine as bright as the sky, and those who lead many to righteousness will shine like the stars forever."
Daniel 12:3

Prayer:
Dear Lord, I will rise and shine in the name of Jesus. This little light of mine. I'm gonna let it shine. You are the light of the world. A city set on a hill cannot be hidden. I will continue to shine in the mighty name of Jesus. Amen.

Affirmation:
I am an expression of divine intelligence.

Day 336: Shine

"Turn us again to Yourself, oh Lord God of Heaven's armies. Make Your face shine down upon us. Only then will we be saved."
Psalm 80:19

Prayer:
Dear Lord, I am thankful for Your divine radiance that shone upon me. May I radiate brightly, so that my loved ones, community, coworkers, and the world at large may see Jesus through me. May the people see the goodness that flows from my heart. In Jesus' Name, Amen.

Affirmation:
Today we shall grow.

Week 49:
Blessings

Day 337: Blessings

"The Lord bless thee and keep thee. The Lord make His face shine upon thee
and be gracious unto thee. The Lord lift up His countenance upon thee and give thee peace."
Numbers 6:24-26

Prayer:
Dear Lord, thank You for blessing me. Bless all of my days on this earth, and bless all of my comings and goings. I pray that You anoint my head with blessings, and make Your face shine upon me. In Jesus' Holy Name, Amen.

Affirmation:
I declare the blessing of the Lord over my family, over my children and grandchildren, in Jesus' Name.

____

Day 338: Blessings

"Blessed are the peacemakers, for they shall be called the children of God."
Matthew 5:19

Prayer:
Dear Lord, You are amazing. Thank You, Lord. You are the Prince of Peace. Thank You for giving me the ministry of reconciliation. Peacemakers are children of God. Blessed are the peacemakers, for they will be called the children of God. Amen.

Affirmation:
I declare that I will represent the Kingdom of God well. I am a peacemaker, in Jesus' Name, Amen.

Day 339: Blessings

"If you obey all the decrees and commands I am giving you today,
all will be well with you and your children. I am giving you these instructions,
so you will enjoy a long life in the land the Lord your God is giving you for all time."
Deuteronomy 4:40

Prayer:
Dear Heavenly Father, I will keep all of Your commandments and follow all of Your instructions. I desire to enjoy a long life in the land of the Lord. Bless me, dear Lord, and cause Your face to shine upon me. In Jesus' Name, Amen.

Affirmation:
I declare that there are benefits when you obey God.

____
____
____
____
____
____
____
____
____

Day 340: Blessings

"Those who listen to instructions will prosper; those who trust the Lord will be joyful."
Proverbs 16:20

Prayer:
Dear Lord Jesus, thank You that Your love and grace towards me is waiting for me as I open my eyes to a brand new day. Your blessings and mercies are new every morning. You are great, and I love You. All I have needed, You have provided. Bless Your Holy Name, Amen.

Affirmation:
I declare that we will follow God's instructions, and the joy of the Lord is our strength.

____
____
____
____
____
____
____
____
____
____
____
____

Day 341: Blessings

"Beloveth, I wish, above all things, that thou mayest prosper and be in health, even as thy soul prospereth."
3 John 1: 1-2

Prayer:
Dear Lord, You are the keeper of my soul. You have blessed me indeed. I am forever thankful for the many blessings that You have granted me. I owe it all to You. In Jesus' Name, Amen.

Affirmation:
I declare divine health and prosperity is mine, in Jesus' Name.

____
____
____
____
____
____
____
____
____
____
____
____
____
____
____
____

Day 342: Blessings

"The blessings of the Lord makes a person rich, and He adds no sorrow with it."
Proverbs 10:22

Prayer:
Dear Lord, thank You for Your many blessings that You have showered over me. I ask You to continue to pour Your bountiful blessing and mercy on me. I ask this in the Marvelous Name of Jesus. Amen.

Affirmation:
I declare multiplications of blessing over your life, in Jesus' Name, Amen.

____
____
____
____
____
____
____
____
____
____
____
____
____

Day 343: Blessings

"The Lord is my shepherd, I shall not want. He maketh me to lie down in green pastures. He leadeth me beside the still waters."
Psalm 23:1-2

Prayer:
Dear Lord, let me be satisfied with favor and filled with Your blessing. I am the seed of Abraham through Jesus Christ, and I receive the blessings of Abraham. Bless me and multiply me as the stars of heaven and as the sand of the shore. In Jesus' Name, Amen.

Affirmation:
I declare that the Good Shepherd takes care of me, in Jesus' Name.

____
____
____
____
____
____
____
____
____
____

Week 50:

The Power of God

Day 344: The Power of God

"For God has not given us a spirit of fear
and timidity, but of power, love, and self-discipline."
2 Timothy 1:7

Prayer:
Dear Lord, we thank You that we have not been given the spirit of fear and timidity. Lord, You have given us power, love, and self-discipline. We can do all things through Christ who strengthens us. The power of the Lord dwells on the inside of us. Today, we honor that our God is all-powerful. Our desire is to fulfill His plans. Not my will, but Your will be done. In Jesus' Name, Amen.

Affirmation:
I am complete in God.

____
____
____
____
____
____
____
____
____
____
____

Day 345: The Power of God

"Yours, oh Lord, is the greatness, the power, the glory, the victory,
and the majesty. Everything in the heavens and on earth is Yours, oh Lord,
and this is Your Kingdom. We adore You as the one who is over all things."
1 Chronicles 29:11

Prayer:
Dear God, You are God Almighty. The only wise God. This is Your Kingdom. We adore You that Your will be done in our lives. We desire to be transformed. A new creature, in Jesus' Name, Amen.

Affirmation:
We are ambassadors for Christ, and we walk in love.

Day 346: The Power of God

"Although He was crucified in weakness, He now lives by the power of God. We too are weak, just as Christ was, but when
we deal with You, we will be alive with Him and will have God's power."
2 Corinthians 13:4

Prayer:
Heavenly Father, when I am weak, You are strong. Our God is wonderful. The same power that is in our Lord and Savior is in us. For the power of our God lives in the inside of us. We will use the authority that has been given to us wisely. In Jesus' Name, Amen.

Affirmation:
My brethren, be strong in the Lord, and in the power of His might.

____
____
____
____
____
____
____
____

Day 347: The Power of God

"But the Lord made the earth by His power, and He preserves it by His wisdom. With His own understanding, he stretched out the heavens."
Jeremiah 10:12

Prayer:
Dear God, You are a miracle working God. You made the earth by Your power, and You preserved it by Your wisdom. So God created man in His own image, in the image of God, created He him. Male and female, created He them. We thank You for Your miraculous power, in Jesus' Name.

Affirmation:
I am made in the image of God.

Day 348: The Power of God

"He telleth the number of the star; He calleth them all by their names.
Great is our Lord and of great power; His understanding is infinite."
Psalm 147:4-5

Prayer:
Our Father, You are amazing. There is no one like you. Everything in heaven and on earth is because of Your spoken words. Your power is great because of Your wisdom. We pray for wisdom in our lives. Lord, bless us with wisdom and understanding, for we need it. In Jesus' Name, Amen.

Affirmation:
Our God is wise and full of wisdom, and we are wise and full of wisdom.

Day 349: The Power of God

"By His divine power, God has given us everything we need for living a godly life. We have received all of this by coming to know Him,
the one who called us to Himself by means of His marvelous glory and excellence."
2 Peter 1:3

Prayer:
Our Father, You have been so good to us. Everything we need, Your hands have provided. You have fearfully and wonderfully made us. The power of God dwells within every born-again believer, and energizes them. Our God is all-powerful. God's power is immeasurable. We give thanks, oh Lord. In Jesus' Name, Amen.

Affirmation:
I am called to be a light of Christ and glorify God.

____
____
____
____
____
____
____
____

Day 350: The Power of God

"For the Kingdom of God is not just a lot of talk; it is living by God's power."
1 Corinthians 4:20

Prayer:
Dear God, the Kingdom of God is not just a lot of talk; it is living by God's power. Our God's power is divine. His divine power has given us everything we need for a godly life through our knowledge of Him who called us by His own glory and goodness. In Jesus' Name, Amen.

Affirmation:
God's divine power has granted us all things that pertain to godliness through the knowledge of Him who called us to His own glory and excellence.

Week 51:
Family

Day 351: Family

"Grandchildren are the crowning glory of the aged; parents are the pride of their children."
Proverbs 17:6

Prayer:
Heavenly Father, we thank You for families all over the world. Help us to consider one another's feelings. Help us to love each other and to forgive quickly. Help us to uplift, encourage, and strengthen one another through fellowship and through Your Word. Amen.

Affirmation:
We will love and appreciate each other every day.

Day 352: Family

"Children are a gift from the Lord; they are a reward from Him."
Psalm 127:3

Prayer:
Dear Lord, my family loves You. We surrender fully to You and pray that Your love will guide us today and every day. We appreciate our children. They are a gift from the Lord. We ask for Your blessing today as we pray these prayers over our children's lives. Lord, we pray that You will keep our children safe. In Jesus' Name, Amen.

Affirmation:
Our family is blessed and highly favored.

____
____
____
____
____
____
____
____
____
____
____
____
____
____

Day 353: Family

"Fathers, do not provoke your children to anger by the way you treat them.
Rather, bring them up with the discipline and instruction that comes from the Lord."
Ephesians 6:4

Prayer:
Dear Lord, we're very thankful to You. Thank You for allowing us to enjoy each other's company. Bless us each day as we seek You. Help the leaders in families to be true disciples of Christ. Surround them with Your favor and protection, and guard them in all their ways. Help us to pray together. In Jesus' Name, Amen.

Affirmation:
We forgive each other and move forward with love and compassion.

____
____
____
____
____
____
____
____

Day 354: Family

"Most important of all, continue to show deep love for each other, for love covers a multitude of sins. Cheerfully share your home with those who need a meal or a place to stay. God has given

each of you a gift from His great variety of spiritual gifts. Use them well to serve one another.

Do you have the gift of speaking? Then speak as though God himself were speaking through you.

Do you have the gift of helping others? Do it with all the strength and energy that God supplies.

Then everything you do will bring glory to God through Jesus Christ.

All glory and power to Him forever and ever! Amen."

1 Peter 4:8-11

Prayer:

Dear Lord, grant us the strength to face life's challenges together as a family. Let us lean on one another and find courage and resilience in times of trial. We thank You in advance for the work You are going to do in their life. In Jesus' Name, Amen.

Affirmation:

I am a member of a loving and supportive family.

Day 355: Family

"Children, obey your parents, because you belong to the Lord, for this is the right thing to do. Honor your father and mother. This is the first commandment with a promise. If you honor your father
and mother, things will go well for you, and you will have a long life on the earth."
Ephesians 6:1-3

Prayer:
Heavenly Father, I thank You that all good gifts come from You. I thank You for my family. Please, guide my children. I pray that You will be Lord over their lives. Please, protect them and order their steps. In Jesus' Name, Amen.

Affirmation:
Our family is strong, united, and supportive.

____

____

____

____

____

____

____

____

____

____

Day 356: Family

"Children, always obey your parents, for this pleases the Lord."
Colossians 3:20

Prayer:
Dear Lord, I will bless Your name forever. I pray that our children will allow You to transform their life. Our children shall know the truth. As adults, we have the responsibility to care for them. I pray that our children will live the full and abundant life God desires for them. In Jesus' Name, Amen.

Affirmation:
My family is a place where I can be vulnerable and honest.

____
____
____
____
____
____
____
____
____
____
____
____
____
____
____
____

Day 357: Family

"Make allowance for each other's faults, and forgive anyone who offends you. Remember, the Lord forgave you, so you must forgive others."

Colossians 3:13

Prayer:

Heavenly Father, we thank You for the gift of family. We are grateful for the love and support we find in one another. May we never take our family for granted and always cherish the moments we have together. Help us to practice love and forgiveness within our family. Amen.

Affirmation:

I love my family with all of my heart.

Week 52:

Honoring Legacy

Day 358: Honoring Legacy

"Thou shall not bow thyself to them nor serve them, for I the Lord thy God
am a jealous God, visiting the iniquity of the fathers upon the children
upon the third and fourth generation of them that hate me. And shewing
mercy unto thousands of them that love me and keep my commandments."

Exodus 20:5-6

Prayer:

Dear Father God, You are the living God. We serve You with all of our being. We ask for Your forgiveness. We thank You for giving us new mercies everyday. We pray that we will be a reflection of Your Son Jesus. In Jesus' Name, Amen.

Affirmation:

It is our responsibility to touch lives and to leave a legacy.

____

____

____

____

____

____

____

Day 359: Honoring Legacy

"Let each generation tell its children of Your mighty acts; let them proclaim Your power.
I will meditate on Your majestic, glorious splendor and Your wonderful miracles."
Psalm 145: 4-5

Prayer:
Dear Lord, let each generation tell its children of Your mighty acts; for the earth is the Lord's, and we see Your wonderful works. Our children will meditate on Your majestic, glorious splendor and your wonderful miracles. Amen.

Affirmation:
Honoring our loved one's legacy and inspiring others to live their legacy too.

____
____
____
____
____
____
____
____
____
____
____

Day 360: Honoring Legacy

"A good man leaveth an inheritance to his children's children. And the wealth of the sinner is laid up for the just."
Proverbs 13:22

Prayer:
Dear Lord, You are concerned about the legacy we leave for our families and future generations. Lord, grant us the desire to leave a legacy that pleases You. We pray that we will be the change and the voice that's needed. In Jesus' Name, Amen.

Affirmation:
We shall live a spiritual life to leave a spiritual legacy.

Day 361: Honoring Legacy

“He that followeth after righteousness and mercy findeth life, righteousness, and honor.”
Hebrews 11:20

Prayer:
Dear Lord, we all have loved ones who have departed this life. Receive their souls. We pray that You will grant them rest. May we reflect on their memories. Their legacy shall forever live through us. Thank You, Lord, for the lives of our loved ones. We are thankful for the time we had together. In Jesus’ Name, Amen.

Affirmation:
We shall cherish our loved ones’ memories and honor their legacy.

Day 362: Honoring Legacy

"Children are a gift from the Lord; they are a reward from Him."
Psalm 127:3

Prayer:

Dear Lord, the best legacy that we can leave our family and loved ones is to live a holy life, a lifestyle that pleases the Lord. We are reminded of the scripture, "Be ye holy as I am holy". We pray that our lives will be pleasing unto You, Lord. Let our lives be a reflection of Christ, then we will surely leave our children a legacy.

Affirmation:

My lifestyle is a reflection of Christ, and that's the legacy that shall be remembered.

____

____

____

____

____

____

____

____

____

____

____

____

Day 363: Honoring Legacy

"Whoever pursues righteousness and unfailing love will find life, righteousness, and honor."
Proverbs 21:21

Prayer:

Dear Lord, we praise You, Lord, for You are holy and righteous. We honor You for being the Great I Am. Our desire is to pursue righteousness. We proclaim Your majesty, giving You all the glory and honor. In Jesus' Name, Amen.

Affirmation:

We shall leave a legacy of righteousness and honor.

Day 364: Honoring Legacy

"For this is how God loved the world: He gave His one and only Son, so that
everyone who believes in Him will not perish but have eternal life. God sent His Son
into the world not to judge the world, but to save the world through Him."
John 3:16-17

Prayer:
Dear Lord, we thank You for Your love. We thank You for eternal life. We shall live a life that pleases You. We shall leave a legacy of love. In Jesus' Name, Amen.

Affirmation:
We shall live to love and leave a legacy of love.

I.

I decided to write this Prayer Journal and Devotional because it was the Word of God that kept me during a very difficult time in my life. My youngest son, at the age of 36, was missing. He was nowhere to be found. Days, weeks, and then months passed. There are thousands of parents that are searching for answers concerning missing loved ones. According to the National Missing and Unidentified Persons (NamUs) database, which is funded by the U.S. Department of Justice, more than 600,000 people go missing annually. Approximately, 4,400 unidentified bodies are recovered each year.

It was the longest night of my life. The search lasted 10 months and 10 days. It was the prayers that sustained me. My prayer is that this Prayer Journal and Devotional encourages you through grief, loss, hope, and recovery.

The grief of child-loss is a journey; nonetheless you can gain the victory.

My prayer is that God will continue to heal the brokenhearted and bind up their wounds.

God is with you in your pain and grief. God will never leave you.
That is a promise He made to us.
He will never forsake us. Trust the Lord when you are facing the challenges of life.
Always remember, our hope is in the Lord.

About The Author

Dr. Patricia L. Harris is a native of Newport News, Virginia. She is a wife, mother, grandmother, and a spiritual mother.

Dr. Patricia L. Harris has an apostolic voice. She has evangelized around the globe for thirty years declaring the Gospel of Jesus Christ. Dr. Patricia L. Harris is a Christian Counselor, Educator, Trauma Informed Coach, Spiritual Life Coach, Mental Health Advocate, Domestic Violence Survivor Advocate, and Homicide Survivor Advocate.

She is the founder of Resilience Life Skill Academy, Loving Kindness Kingdom Global Alliance, Women With A Vision Ministries, and Mothers Against Violence, Inc.

She is an author and has a heart of compassion. She has endured much. Her favorite Scripture is Romans 8:18, "For I consider that the sufferings of this present time are not worth comparing with the glory that is to be revealed to us".

www.ingramcontent.com/pod-product-compliance
Lightning Source LLC
Chambersburg PA
CBHW060922120626
46557CB00003B/839
* 9 7 9 8 9 8 6 8 6 2 0 9 5 *